MAQBOOL

The Original Screenplay
(with English translation)

Vishal Bhardwaj
with Abbas Tyrewala

HarperCollins *Publishers* India

First published in India in 2014 by
HarperCollins *Publishers* India

HarperCollins Publishers India, Cyber City, Building 10-A, Gurugram,
Haryana-122002, India
www.harpercollins.co.in

2 4 6 8 10 9 7 5 3 1

P-ISBN: 978-93-5029-807-7
E-ISBN: 978-93-5029-808-4

Typeset in Sabon 11/14 and Shiva 12.5/14.5 at
Saanvi Graphics Noida

Printed and bound at
MicroPrints India, New Delhi D

MIX
Paper
FSC
FSC™ C218906

This product is made of FSC®-certified and other controlled material.

HarperCollins Publishers, Macken House, 39/40 Mayor Street
Upper, Dublin 1, D01 C9W8, Ireland

MAQBOOL

Vishal Bhardwaj is a critically acclaimed Hindi film director, writer, screenwriter, producer, music composer and playback singer. Born in Bijnore and raised in Meerut in Uttar Pradesh, Bhardwaj studied at Hindu College, University of Delhi. Known for his collaboration with filmmaker and lyricist Gulzar – he shot into fame when he scored the music for Gulzar's *Maachis* – Bhardwaj has directed such films as *Kaminey*, *7 Khoon Maaf* and *Matru ki Bijli ka Mandola*. *Maqbool*, adapted from *Macbeth*, is part of a trilogy of films based on Shakespeare's plays directed by Bhardwaj, the other two being *Omkara* (adapted from *Othello*) and *Haider* (adapted from *Hamlet*).

Preface

It was a five-hour-long train journey from Dehradun to Delhi. I was escorting my godson Aalaap back from his boarding school in the summer holidays. Out of boredom I asked for any book of short stories from his course books and he pulled out this abridged version of Shakespeare's plays by Lamb. The first story I read was *Macbeth*. Suddenly Kurosawa's *Throne of Blood* came rushing back and within minutes of reaching the part about Duncan's killing, I had decided to adapt *Macbeth* to Mumbai's underworld.

Before this I honestly had no interest in the work of Shakespeare or, for that matter, in that of any other English literary figure. I had a brief encounter with Shakespeare's work in school, where I had read *The Merchant of Venice*. But that's all.

I began my carrier as a music composer with the film *Maachis* by Gulzar Saab. It was an overnight success that put me amongst the topmost music composers of the late 1990s. But as I pursued my carrier further, I found myself creatively frustrated with the kind of films I was being offered as a music director. I was slowly going out of work. Somewhere I sensed that unless I did something out of the box, my good days were over. So I decided to become a director and secretly nurtured the craft of screenwriting for years by reading books.

During the preparation for my first directorial venture *Makdee*, a film for children, I happened to see Akira Kurosawa's masterpiece *Throne of Blood*, which was the Japanese adaptation of *Macbeth*. It remained stuck in my subconscious forever after that.

Like every filmmaker I also wanted to explore the juiciest genre of cinema – the world of gangsters. I was looking for a story that could give me the scope to have the underworld as the backdrop but with a strong human story. During this period, whatever I read, any story or article, I read it with only one agenda in mind – to find a story for my gangster film. Which I accidently stumbled upon in a child's schoolbook.

As soon as I alighted from the train in Delhi I made a call to my cowriter Abbas Tyrewala and threw the *Macbeth* bomb on him. He went quiet for a moment and then whispered 'Gurujan ho gaya.'

We ordered the full play from the school book shop and went through it many a time before we began to work out our screenplay.

The first breakthrough in the screenplay was the discovery of witches in our story. What could have made the best parallel to the witches in contemporary India? Of course, cops. But the major decision was to change the character of Lady Macbeth – from Macbeth's wife to Duncan's mistress who was having an affair with Macbeth. This changed the dynamics of the relationships completely. Suddenly the sexual conflict became the core of the screenplay. For Macbeth, the Lady Macbeth became the throne herself.

While we were writing the screenplay we had no idea that one day it will be so minutely judged, scrutinized and admired all over the world. We were ignorant and didn't expect to be taken so seriously. Perhaps this ignorance was the primary reason that made us unafraid to take any kind of liberty we felt was fit for our screenplay and probably that's what made it special too.

It was such a difficult task to find a financier to make the film. It took me almost two years till Bobby Bedi read it accidently and recognized the potential of the script. By that time nearly all the stars and producers had rejected it for some reason or the other. And thank God they did because only Irrfan Khan could be my *Maqbool*.

When I look back at the journey of my creative life I feel like some supernatural character of the Bard's play itself. No one, including me, would have ever thought in their wildest dreams that some day I would be writing the preface of a book based on a film adapted from a Shakespeare's play. At times like these your head bows down in humility to thank the Almighty for being so kind.

The film was shot in fifty days – thirty-five days in Bhopal and the rest in Mumbai between March and May of 2003. It was released a year later in January 2004. It couldn't even recover its cost at the box office but was greatly admired by the critics. Though it was a great success in the international festival circuit, it somehow could not reach the theaters overseas.

In order to shoot at the desired locations in Bhopal, I had to let go of my salary for being the writer, director and music director. For years I kept cribbing about the fact that I did not make a single rupee out of it but today when I sit back and think, a shiver of fear runs through my spine when I mull over what would have happened to me if I hadn't made *Maqbool*. Surely, I would not have had the same respect for myself that I do today.

9 September 2014 **Vishal Bhardwaj**
Mumbai

SC. 1

EXT. /NIGHT/POLICE VAN

On the vaporized surface of a glass, a finger makes a horoscope, while on the soundtrack we hear the laughter of a cop (Inspector Purohit) and a gangster (Saadiq Chikna), the sound of heavy rains, and urgent summons on the radio of the police van.

INSP. PUROHIT
(holding the laughter)

सारी रात की माँ बहन कर दी साले ने... जब भी घोड़ा खींचे साला रोने लगे जोर से... मेलया... अरे उतने नजदीक से गोली मारेंगे तो साली इनक्वायरी बैठ जाएगी ना हम पे... भागने को बोला तो घुटने में घुस गया पोपट... बड़ा मुश्किल है डरे हुए का इनकाउन्टर करना... अब रोते हुए को कैसे मारेगा कोई... हैं? हँसते-हँसते आओ हँसते-हँसते जाओ...

Sonuvabitch screwed up my whole night… everytime I'd cock the gun, he'd start screaming… shooting him in the back was out of the question… asked him to run but the bugger fell on my knees grovelling… it's damn tough to shoot a guy who's shitting fear like that… mostly I like the ones who 'easy come, easy go'…

SAADIQ

लेकिन था कौन साब?

But who was it?

INSP. PUROHIT

जाने दो ना... बारह बज गये क्या?

Forget it… Is it twelve yet?

Saadiq checks his watch.

SAADIQ

नई... टाइम है... बताओ ना साब... था कौन?

No… there's time… tell me… who was it?

INSP. PANDIT

नाटा...

Nata…

Pandit has finished drawing the horoscope on the glass. Saadiq's face suddenly drops. Purohit and Saadiq are in the back of the van drinking. Purohit turns to Pandit.

INSP. PUROHIT

किसके भविष्य मे उंगली कर रहे हो पंडित जी...?

Whose fate are you fingering, Panditji?

INSP. PANDIT

मुंबई...

Mumbai's…

SAADIQ

साब नाटा...

What happened to Nata?

Purohit ignores him.

INSP. PUROHIT
(to Pandit)

अच्छा ये... मुंबई की पत्री है ये... (*laughs*) क्या लिखा है मुंबई के भविष्य में...

This is Mumbai's horoscope… (*laughs*) What does it say?

SAADIQ

साब नाटा...

Sir… Nata… ?

Purohit suddenly stops laughing and turns to Saadiq.

INSP. PUROHIT

नाटा गया... गया...

Nata's history…

Fear creeps into Saadiq's eyes.

SAADIQ

कब...?

When?

INSP. PUROHIT

कल... आज कोई और जाईंगा... ओए बारह बजे क्या?

Last night… and today somebody else's going to get lucky… Is it twelve yet?

SAADIQ

आप लोग अब्बा जी के आदमी हो...

You guys work for Abba ji?

INSP. PANDIT

तु भी तो मुगल की औरत है... चिकने...

Just like you are Mughal's bitch, Princess...

They both laugh... Tears emerge in Saadiq's eyes.

SAADIQ

साब मुझे मारना मत साब...

Don't kill me, please...

INSP. PUROHIT

ऐ... रो मत...

Don't you dare cry!

Saadiq holds Purohit's feet, and starts crying.

INSP. PUROHIT

पैर को हाथ मत लगा... साले धंधा करना जानता नहीं है... चुप...

Stop that... Bastard, don't you know how to play by the rules...

INSP. PANDIT

धंधे का पहला असूल याद है? कि भूल गया...

What's the first rule of this business?

SAADIQ

(crying)

फैमली मेमबर को टारगेट नहीं करते... साब...

Family members are not to be targeted...

Purohit grabs him by the hair.

INSP. PUROHIT

तो फिर इधर देख... उपर देख... काहे को उड़ाया अब्बा जी के भाई को?

तेरे को क्या लगा? मियाँ कम्पनी की छीर जाएगी?

Then… why the fuck did your gang kill Abba ji's brother? What did you guys think? Miyan's gang will take this lying down.

INSP. PANDIT

बारह बजे चालीसमा खतम हो रहा है... सुवह तक तुम्हारी फैमली finished… 'The End'…

The mourning period ends at midnight… By morning, all of you will be dead… 'The End'…

INSP. PUROHIT

कहाँ छुपा है मुगल बता दे... बता दे बच जाएगा... मियाँ ने जबान दी है...

Just tell us where Mughal is hiding… we'll let you go… Miyan's given his word.

Saadiq keeps on howling as Pandit continues.

INSP. PUROHIT

सुन... सुन... रो मत रो मत (Purohit lifts Saadiq's face)… सुन पंडित की कोई भविष्यवाणी गलत नई होती... पूछ मुंबई की पत्री मे किसका नाम लिखा है... अब्बा जी या मुगल का?

Now stop crying and listen (Purohit lifts Saadiq's face)… This learned man has never made a false prediction in his life… Ask him… who the next king of the city is… Abba ji or Mughal?

INSP. PANDIT

मक़बूल... मियाँ मक़बूल...

Maqbool… Mian Maqbool.

SC. 2

Introduction of Maqbool. An extended opening credit sequence. One by one Maqbool, Kaka and Surti finish off important underworld figureheads. After the last killing Maqbool dials his mobile.

SC. 2A

Purohit picks up the phone in van. Saadiq is now sitting on the bench having his drink. He now looks a little relaxed.

INSP. PUROHIT

हाँ मियाँ... आदाब...

Ya Miyan... Greetings...

SC. 2B

Cut to Maqbool, now in a van followed by two more vans behind. Conversation is intercut between Purohit and Maqbool. Kaka is sitting by Maqbool's side while Guddu is on the driving seat.

MAQBOOL

मुगल कहाँ है...?

Where's Mughal?

SC. 2C

INSP. PUROHIT

वो कहता है वो आप ही को बताएगा... ले बात कर

He wants to tell you himself...

He passes the phone to Saadiq.

SAADIQ

हाँ मियाँ सालां वालेकुम...

(He keeps quiet for a while)...

Greetings Miyan... ya...

MAQBOOL

कहाँ है मुगल?

Where's Mughal?

SAADIQ

गोरई में, बंगले पे...

Mughal's in the bungalow in Gorai...

MAQBOOL

और बोटी...?

And Boti... ?

SAADIQ

वो बोरिवली में अपने ससुराल पे मियाँ...

Borivali... at his in-laws.

SC. 3

INT. /NIGHT/VAN

Maqbool puts a hand on Guddu's shoulder. Guddu stops the vehicle.

MAQBOOL

बाप गोरई बेटा बोरिवली... (*Maqbool looks at Kaka*) मैं मुगल को लेता हूं तुम लोग बोटी के यहाँ जाओ...

The father is in Gorai and the son's in Borivali... (*Maqbool looks at Kaka*) I'll go look up the old guy... you guys sniff out the son.

Guddu interrupts.

GUDDU

मै जाऊंगा मुगल के यहाँ...

Why can't I go get Mughal...?

Maqbool gives Kaka and Surti an annoyed look.

KAKA
(to Guddu)
अबे जो कहा जाय बस वो किया कर समझा...
Just do what you're told.

Maqbool gets out of the car.

GUDDU
ठीक है तो तू भी जा उसके साथ...
Thanks a lot, Dad… I can manage on my own… why don't you also go with him?

Kaka hits him on his neck.

KAKA
क्यूँ बे मेरे सामने शर्म आएगी उसे गोली मारने मे...
Why? You'll feel shy pulling the trigger in front of me?

GUDDU
ठीक है मै जाता हूँ मियाँ के साथ...
Fine… I'll go with Miyan then.

Guddu tries to get up but Kaka stops him and gets out of the car. Guddu zips off.

KAKA
(shouts)
ध्यान रखियो बे...
Be safe…

MAQBOOL
(smiles)

तेरा बेटा नहीं बाप है वो... चल...

Come on… he's not a child anymore…

Cut back to van.

SC. 4

EXT. /INT. /NIGHT/POLICE VAN ON A HIGHWAY DHABA

Purohit is pouring a drink in Saadiq's glass who looks quite drunk by now.

SAADIQ

अरे बस बस पुरोहित साब... बस...

Not any more, Purohit sir.

INSP. PUROHIT

अरे पी चिकने पी... मौज कर आज तेरी 15 अगस्त है...

Drink up Princess. Let it flow tonight… tonight you've got freedom…

SAADIQ

नवम्बर में 15 अगस्त कैसे होगी साब... क्या साब...

Freedom from what, sir?

INSP. PANDIT

अरे मुगल के बिस्तर से आजाद हुआ है ना तू....

From Mughal's bedroom, that's what, sweetheart.

Pandit chuckles. Saadiq is embarrassed.

INSP. PUROHIT

और वैसे... लौंडेबाजी का शौक ना अब्बा जी को है ना मियाँ को...

You'll be safe here. Neither Abba ji nor Miyan is into boys…

INSP. PUROHIT

और ना हमें…

and neither are we…

Purohit and Pandit laugh and Saadiq joins them. Suddenly Purohit takes out his gun and shoots Saadiq from point blank range. The blood splashes on the horoscope made on the glass van. Pandit reacts with a jerk.

INSP. PANDIT

देख के मारा कर यार, सारी मुंबई खून से भर दी…

What the hell!… you've spilt blood all over my city.

Cut on the blood streaming on the horoscope.

SC. 5

INT. /NIGHT/MUGHAL'S BUNGALOW

Maqbool and Kaka tower over a cowering Mughal. Maqbool asks him one last time.

MAQBOOL

बोल मुगल, हमारे लोगों में से किसने गद्दारी की थी, नाम बोल…

Who was your man in our gang?

Mughal is unfazed.

MUGHAL

तूने…

You… you were the traitor.

Maqbool smirks and pulls the trigger. Nothing fires. He shoots again. Nothing happens. Kaka starts laughing. Maqbool dumps the gun down the commode and leaves. Kaka can't stop laughing. Finally, Thapa, Maqbool's man, finishes off Mughal.

SC. 5A

INT. /NIGHT/ABBA JI'S ROOM

Abba ji picks up the phone in the middle of the night. We see the glimpse of a young lady sleeping by his side. Cut to Maqbool.

SC. 6

INT. /NIGHT/VAN

Asif, Abba ji's brother-in-law, picks up the phone.

KAKA

हाँ रे आसिफ हाँ जरा अब्बा जी को दे...

Asif... where's Abba ji?

ASIF

छोटी के कमरे में है जीजू...

He's in Sameera's room.

KAKA

हाँ तो बुला उन्हें...

Go call him...

ASIF

क्या खबर है?

Got some news?

KAKA

अबे तुझ से बोला ना बुला उन्हें...

Call him...

ASIF

अबे कहा ना छोटी को बुखार है... जीजू जान ले लेगा अगर दरवाजा खटकाया तो...

The girl's not well… He'll skin me alive if I knock…

KAKA

अच्छा तो बोलना के हम लोग पनवेल मे हैं... बाहर निकलने के साथ ही फार्म हाउस फोन करना...

Fine… tell him we're headed to the farmhouse… to call back when when he has the time…

ASIF

रूक रूक... मुगल गया क्या?

Wait… Mughal's gone or what?

KAKA

हाँ गया...

Ya…

Asif squeals with delight.

ASIF

और अपना बोटी?

And Boti…?

CUT TO:

SC.7

INT. /NIGHT/BOTI' S PLACE

Guddu pushes Boti's wife, who is crying at his feet, away. Boti is stting on the floor, badly beaten up. One of Guddu's men is holding Boti's small kid who is also howling for his father. Guddu pulls the trigger, but stops as Boti's kid calls:

BOTI'S KID

अब्बू...

Dad...

Guddu can't take his crying anymore.

GUDDU

बाहर ले जाओ बच्चे को...

Take the blasted kid outside...

Guddu can't get himself to shoot. He lifts Boti's face with the pistol.

GUDDU

काम करेगा हमारे साथ...

Will you work for us?

Boti shuts his eyes in affirmation.

CUT TO:

SC.8

INT. /NIGHT/FARMHOUSE

Purohit, Pandit, Maqbool and Kaka are drinking and lolling about, after a hard night's work. Pandit is making horoscope figures on the tray using chicken bone and chutney. Kaka is rolling about the floor laughing.

KAKA

साला इश्क और मियाँ को? मियाँ और लौंडिया??! अच्छा और क्या मिलेगा मियाँ को?

Miyan… and girls?! Miyan… and love?! Fuck me! So what else is Miyan going to inherit?

Pandit looks up from the horoscope.

INSP. PANDIT

साढ़े साती उतरी है तेरी आज से... जो चाहे मिलेगा... जो चाहेगा...

His bad patch has just cleared… he'll get whatever he wants… whatever…

KAKA

जैसे?

For example…?

INSP. PANDIT

बॉलीवुड...

Bollywood…

Kaka cracks up again. Even Maqbool reacts with amusement.

KAKA

बॉलीवुड है अब्बा जी के साले का... वो आसिफ आ जायेगा जीजू-जीजू करते हुए अभी... जीजू... जीजू...

That's Abba ji's brother-in-law's turf. That Asif… nobody's getting that in a hurry… he'll go whining to Abba ji…

Pandit walks over to Kaka with his horoscope tray. Kaka sits up attentively.

INSP. PANDIT

दशम स्थान में शुक्र बलवान है... राजयोग कहते हैं इसे... बालीवुड छोड़... छे महीने मे अब्बा जी की गद्दी मियाँ की है...

Your comet has entered the seventh house in Venus… this normally signifies the king's reign… Forget

Bollywood... in six months' time, Abba ji's own throne will be Miyan's to claim.

Everybody goes silent. Maqbool looks passive.

Pandit raises his hand in the air to anoint.

INSP. PANDIT
'King of Kings'

Purohit shouts at him.

INSP. PUROHIT
अय अय चुप साले...
Shut your trap... you sonuvabitch...

Maqbool is not amused anymore.

MAQBOOL

पंडित तेरे इस चौपधखाने मे विश्वास होता ना तो आज मैं तेरी जबान काट डालता...

If I believed in any of your mumbo jumbo, Pandit… I'd have sliced your tongue off today.

INSP. PUROHIT

काट दो मियाँ काट दो... काट दो... साला इसकी जबान से जो निकलता है सच होता है... अभी-अभी छे महीने पहले बैठे बैठे ऐसे ही मुझसे बोला के तेरी वो पड़ोसन है ना उससे जरा बच कर रहना... एडस मे मरेगी... हट्टी कट्टी... भरी भरी... साली पाँच महीने मे आफ हो गई...

Slice it off, Miyan… whatever he says always comes out to be true. Six months back, he tells me… your neighbour's going to die of AIDS… stay away from her… what do I tell you Miyan… this healthy buxom woman… goes out like that… in five months' flat…

INSP. PANDIT

अहसान मान तेरी जान बचाई साले...

You should be grateful, wretch. I saved your life.

Purohit throws a chicken bone at Pandit who ducks deftly.

Pandit continues bitching to Miyan.

INSP. PANDIT

मियाँ ये हफ्ता लेना भूल जाता था पर रोजाना लेनी नहीं भूलता था...

He'd forget his weekly commission… but he wouldn't forget to visit hers truly everyday.

Everybody laughs. The tension defuses.

INSP. PUROHIT

हँस रहे हो मियाँ... काली जबान है साले की बता रहा हूँ...

You people are laughing now… but this guy's got one helluva black tongue.

Pandit sticks his tongue out. Kaka laughs and asks Pandit, pointing to the second horoscope on the table.

KAKA

अच्छा एक काम करो... छोड़ो उस को पंडितजी... आप कुछ मेरे बारे मे बतलाओ... जरा बढ़िया सा... आराम से टाइम ले के...

Any forecasts for me, Panditji?

Pandit studies his chart carefully.

INSP. PANDIT

अरे... कमाल है... तू अभी तक जिंदा कैसे है?

Remarkable! It's a miracle you're still alive…

Everyone laughs again. Kaka is not amused. He gets up to make himself a drink.

KAKA

चुप बे... साली हँसने की क्या बात है उसमें? साले मियाँ से कम नही उड़ाये होंगे गिन लो आज के मिला के...

Shut your mouth… all of you. I mustn't have killed any less than Miyan… ya… and that includes tonight's.

Pandit tries to humour him.

INSP. PANDIT

तेरे बेटे की पत्री देखी... बहुत दम है साले में...

I've seen your son's chart… that lad has great promise.

INSP. PUROHIT

वैसे मियाँ जी का जवाब है तेरा बेटा...

He's the next Miyan in the making for sure...

Maqbool reacts to this. Suddenly the phone rings. Kaka picks it up, there is no response. The phone rings again, this time Maqbool picks it up.

SC. 8A

INT. /NIGHT/BALCONY OF A BUNGLOW

A female whose face is not visible asks in a very hushed tone.

VOICE

तुम ठीक हो ना...

Are you ok?

Cut to Maqbool

SC. 9

INT. /NIGHT/FARM HOUSE

Maqbool is awkward as everybody is intrigued by the call.

MAQBOOL

हाँ... ठीक हूँ...

Hmm... I'm fine...

Lady on the other side hangs up. Maqbool turns, Kaka smiles.

KAKA

वाह रे पंडित तू सही कह रहा था यार... तो वाकइ है बे... आये मियाँ...
कौन है भाई...

So Miyan's really in love… who's this latest squeeze now?

MAQBOOL

उनकी पडोसन... बुलाऊँ...

Purohit's neighbour… should I call her? You'll take hers?

Maqbool and Purohit clap and laugh, while Pandit smiles. Purohit's mobile rings.

INSP. PUROHIT

Hello… कौन देवसरे... थाने मे फोन करो सुबह...

Hello… Devsare? Devsare who? Call me in the morning.

He disconnects. The phone rings again.

INSP. PANDIT

ले तू बात कर यार... इंगलिश बात करता है साला...

Here… you speak to him… Idiot speaks only in English…

He disconnects.

INSP. PUROHIT

देवसरे... कौन है ये देवसरे?

Who the hell is this Devsare?

Pandit shrugs his shoulders.

MAQBOOL

तुम लोगों क़ा नया ACP…

The new Assistant Commissioner of Police…

Cut to the shocked faces of Purohit and Pandit.

SC. 10

EXT. /DAY/MUGHAL'S HIDEOUT

Devsare gets down from the official car. Insp. Pandit and Purohit salute him. A plain-clothes man whispers something into Devsare's ear. Devsare enters the bungalow, Pandit and Purohit follow him. Lots of dead bodies, covered in white sheets, are in the premises. Crime and forensic photographers are flashing their camera on the walls and floor covered with dry blood stains.

DEVSARE

काफी सुना है आप लोगों के बारे में...

I've heard a lot about you two...

DEVSARE

किस का हाथ है इसमें...?

Who's behind these killings?

INSP. PUROHIT

पुलिस का नहीं है sir...

Not us, sir.

Pandit smiles, Devsare gives a stern look.

DEVSARE

Crime के वक़्त आप दोनो कहाँ थे...?

Where were you at the time of the killings?

INSP. PUROHIT

ड्यूटी पर सर...

On duty sir...

DEVSARE

ड्यूटी पर... ड्यूटी पर होते तो शायद ये crime होता ही नहीं...

This wouldn't have happened if you had been on duty...

INSP. PANDIT

फिर तो बहुत बड़ा crime हो जाता सर... शक्ति का संतुलन बहुत जरूरी है संसार मे सर...

Something worse would have happened, sir... power is a game of exquisite balance...

Devsare turns to Pandit.

INSP. PUROHIT

आग के लिये पानी का डर बना रहना चाहिए... बिना कुछ किए बैठे बिठाए पूरे एक गैंग का सफाया हो गया... सर...

You need water to balance out the fire... A whole gang got wiped out without raising a finger... sir...

INSP. PUROHIT

और जो बचा है वो हमारे साथ है...

... and the one that's left is with us...

Devsare's expression changes, Purohit fumbles.

INSP. PANDIT

मतलब हमारे under है... एक गैंग को control करना ज्यादा आसान है सर...

He means, within our control... It's far easier to control one gang, sir...

DEVSARE

क्या नाम है?

Whose gang?

INSP. PUROHIT

अब्बा जी...

Abba ji's...

DEVSARE

मैने रिश्ता नहीं नाम पूछा है...

I asked for his name, not his title...

SC. 11

INT. /DAY/OFFICE OF DEVSARE

Pandit hands over a file to Devsare. Montage of old newspaper cuttings showing the growth of Abba ji from a small-time gangster to the big don of Mumbai. We hear the V/O in Pandit's voice.

INSP. PANDIT

जहाँगीर खान... लाला जी भाई का दाहिना हाथ था... Gold smuggling से शुरूआत की और लाल जी भाई की मौत के बाद

contract killing और जमीन के गैर कानूनी कब्जों को खाली कराने का धंधा... Minorities के खुदा हैं वो... जिस पार्टी के साथ अब्बा जी हाथ मिला लें वो कभी election नहीं हारती...

Jahangir Khan… he was Lalji Bhai's right hand. Started as a small-time gold smuggler and after Lalji Bhai's death, flourished through contract killings and forcible land eviction. The minorities worship him… whichever political party Abba ji backs is sure to win the polls…

DEVSARE

कोई FIR…

Any FIR… ?

Purohit shows one in the file.

INSP. PUROHIT

जी है... 12 साल पहले... Arrest करने की कोशिश हुई तो शहर में फसाद हो गया...

One… twelve years back… attempts to arrest him resulted in riots all over the city…

SC. 13

EXT. /DAY/KABRISTAAN

A black Mercedes escorted by a few vans stops. Abba ji gets down and walks in along with Maqbool, Kaka, Guddu, Asif and lots of gunmen. The preparations for the burial are going on in the background. Abba ji hugs Boti.

ABBA JI

अल्लाह तौफीक दे... वालिद के साये का कोई सानी नहीं है मियाँ...

May Allah have mercy… it's an irreparable loss…

Boti looks around at Maqbool, Kaka, Guddu and Asif. He looks quite broken by his father's death.

BOTI

किये की कीमत तो चुकाना ही पड़ती है... आपका पनाहगीर हूँ अब्बा जी...

One has to pay for one's deeds... You are all I have left, Abba ji.

He picks up a small boy in his lap.

ABBA JI

ज़ख्म भरने में वक़्त तो लगेगा मियाँ... आपके वालिद और हमारे भाई फना हुए हैं...

Be strong... these wounds take time to heal... your father and my brother are both lying under the same earth...

Boti reacts strongly to this statement. Fear emerges in his eyes. Abba ji looks straight into his eyes.

ABBA JI

हम तो आज तक बेखबर हैं के भाई का खूनी कौन था...?

Till date, I don't know the name of the bloody rat who betrayed us...

Abba ji asks again.

ABBA JI

हम में से कौन था?

Who was the traitor?

Boti slowly turns and looks at Asif... just then the grave is filled and the maulavi starts reciting the 'ziyarat' for the dead. All of them hold up their hand and close eyes, except Asif, who is sweating profusely. Dissolve from his face to his photograph at Abba ji's place.

SC. 14

INT. /DAY/ABBA JI'S HAVELI

Abba ji quietly turns over the pages of a photo album as Asif sits nearby on the floor, crying. A gun is kept on the table, its metal shining in the light.

ABBA JI

निकाह पे नौ एक साल का था तू... मरते वक़्त अमानत के तौर पे छोड़ गयी थी तुझे रूखसाना... अमानत में खयानत नहीं होती मियाँ...

You were not more than nine at the time of the wedding... Rukhsana left you behind as her only living memory... and memories are not to be trifled with...

Abba ji crumples the page from the album. Asif cries even more.

ASIF

जीजू मैं दुबई चला जाउंगा जीजू...

I'll go away to Dubai, brother-in-law…

ABBA JI

एक ही रास्ता है... और एक ही को जाना है... गोली मार हमें...

There's only one journey left to make… and only one of us is booked to go… Shoot me…

ASIF

नहीं जीजू...

No… I can't…

ABBA JI

आसिफ गोली मार...

Shoot me, Asif…

ASIF

नहीं जीजू नहीं...

No… don't do this, please…

ABBA JI
(hollers)

आसिफ...

Asif…

Asif picks up the gun and points it at Abba ji. His hands are shaking.

SC. 14 A

INT. /DAY/ABBA JI'S HAVELI

Downstairs in the porch Maqbool, Kaka and Guddu react to the sound of gunfire. They rush upstairs, to find a dead Asif.

SC. 15

INT./NIGHT/MEETING ROOM

Abba ji sits at the head of the table while Maqbool and the other gang members sit around it. Pandit and Purohit are also there. Maqbool leans over and whispers.

MAQBOOL

मौका मिलते ही फन मारेगा बोटी...

Boti will hit back at the first opportunity…

ABBA JI

पनाह दी... तो दी...

I've spared him his life… once and for all…

Chinna, a prominent gang member, tries to protest.

ABBA JI

जहाँगीर अपनी जबान से नहीं फिरता... मसला ख़त्म... बोटी को कोई हाथ नहीं लगायेगा... और कुछ?

I can't go back on my word... Discussion over... No one will touch Boti... Anything else?

Tawde, another business associate, speaks up.

TAWDE

फिल्म इंडस्ट्री का क्या होगा? कौन देखेगा अभी?

What about the film industry? Who'll look after that now?

Guddu coughs, trying to attract attention to himself. Abba ji chews his paan quietly.

ABBA JI

मक़बूल...

Maqbool...

Maqbool is surprised. To say the least.

MAQBOOL

अब्बा जी मुझसे नहीं होगा... मैं... मैं क्या करूंगा फिल्म इंन्डस्ट्री?

What will I do there, Abba ji?

ABBA JI

अब्बू का नाम सँभालो बेटा... आसिफ ने बहुत कालिख पोती है वहाँ...

Restore our good name, son... Asif's dragged it through much mud.

Abba ji leaves. Maqbool looks back at Pandit and Purohit with amazement. Who in turn look heavenwards.

INT. /NIGHT/ABBA JI'S HAVELI

The dinner. The 'handi' of biryani is kept in the middle of a Dastarkhan, and everybody is sitting around having the meal. Nimmi and Sameera are serving. Bhosle calls out to Nimmi.

BHOSLE

निम्मी भाभी... आप इस बिरयानी की रेसीपी जरूर लिखकर दीजिए हमें...
पेट भर गया नीयत नहीं भरती...

Sister... you must hand me the recipe of this delicious biryani... I'll eat up my fingers up at this rate...

NIMMI

नियाज के खाने की लज़्ज़त ही अलग होती है...

This food is blessed by Allah himself...

She serves some to Abba ji.

ABBA JI

बस बीबा बस... मर जायेंगे हम तो...

I'll burst a gut, dear… no more…

Nimmi goes inside.

NANNY

सेवइयों के लिए जगह रखिएगा आप लोग...

Please keep some space for the sweets…

BHOSLE

नहीं भाई अब और कुछ नहीं...

I can't eat a thing more…

SAMEERA

अंकल मैने बनायी हैं...

Uncle… I've made it with my own hand.

Abba ji hugs Sameera.

ABBA JI

रूखसाना का रस है छोटी के हाथ में...

This little one here cooks just like her mother.

Sameera gets annoyed.

ABBA JI

अच्छा भाई छोटी नहीं... समीरा के हाथ में... सबको खानी पड़ेगी...

I know… I know… You're not so little anymore…
Bring on the dessert! We'll all have to eat then…

GUDDU

और तारीफ भी करनी पड़ेगी...

And then praise it... in that order...

Everybody laughs and Kaka hits Guddu lovingly. Suddenly Abba ji coughs and there is no water in the glass. Maqbool runs inside to get some from the kitchen. Nimmi is inside.

MAQBOOL

पानी...

Water...

Nimmi gives him the glass and suddenly holds Maqbool's hand.

NIMMI

आजकल तुझे प्यास नहीं लगती मियाँ...

You don't feel thirsty nowadays, Miyan...

Maqbool looks at her inviting, mischievous eyes, shakes off her hand and runs out.

CUT TO:

SE. 16

EXT. /NIGHT/ABBA JI'S HAVELI

Everybody is in the balcony. The paans are being served. Abba ji makes one of his special ones for Bhosle.

ABBA JI

कोई देवसरे है...

There is some new cop on the block called Devsare...

BHOSLE

पहली पोस्टिंग है उसकी... अब नया मुसलमान तो पाँचों वक़्त की नमाज़ पढ़ता ही है अब्बा जी...

Ya... its his first posting... He likes flashing his new toys...

CHINNA

साब तीन लोगों का इनकाउन्टर कर दिया है... एक हफ्ते में...

Sir, he's shot three of our men in the last week alone...

Abba ji introduces Chinna and Tawde to Bhosle.

ABBA JI

ये चिन्ना है और से तावड़े... पनवेल और थाने में हमारा काम देखते हैं...

This is Chinna and this is Tawde... They look after our businesses in Panvel and Thane...

Bhosle changes the topic. He addresses Maqbool.

BHOSLE

और मियाँ? बॉलीवुड के क्या हाल है?

So Miyan… how's Bollywood treating you?

MAQBOOL

आप हाल हमारे पूछिये… रज़िया फँस गई है गुन्डों में…

Don't ask. It's like being caught in a den of thieves…

Everybody laughs as Maqbool vents a little steam.

MAQBOOL

घटिया फिल्में… घटिया लोग…

Slimy people, even slimier films…

KAKA

तू अब्बा जी की लाइफ के उपर पिक्चर बनवा के देख… उतरे नही उतरेगी…

You make a film on Abba ji… it'll be an all-time blockbuster.

Nimmi taunts Maqbool.

NIMMI

कोई हिरोइन पसन्द नहीं आयी?

Or better still… find yourself a nice wholesome actress.

Everyone laughs.

KAKA

वो पहले से फिट है भाभी…

He's already been at work on that…

NIMMI

अच्छा... कौन है भाई जिसने पत्थर में पौधा उगा दिया...

Not bad! Who's caused flowers to bloom in this desert?

Everyone laughs again. Maqbool is embarrassed.

MAQBOOL

अब्बा जी बोटी किसी से मिलाने की बात कर रहा था...

Abba ji, Boti wants to set up a meeting...

Nimmi rags him further .

NIMMI

बात मत पलटो मियाँ... कौन है...?

Don't evade the topic, Miyan. Who's the girl?

Maqbool avoids her gaze.

MAQBOOL

तो कल बुलवा लूँ?

Should I call him tomorrow?

Abba ji gives the go-ahead. Nimmi protests.

NIMMI

जहाँगीर कल दरगाह जाना है हमें...

Jahangir, I need to go visit the shrine tomorrow.

ABBA JI

बीबा... आप मन्नतें बहुत माँगते हैं...

You pray too much, dear...

She looks at Maqbool.

NIMMI

पूरी तो एक भी नहीं होती...

If only somebody listens to them...

Maqbool lowers his gaze.

KAKA

होगी भाभी सारी पूरी होगी... अब्बा जी अगर इस साल निम्मी भाभी की पिक्चर नहीं बनवायी ना तो सच बोलता हूँ ठीक नहीं होगा... बोलो भाभी कौन डायरेक्टर चाहिए... करन जौहर, सुभाष घई या अपना क्या कहते हैं राम गोपाल वर्मा... बोलो...

Don't you worry, sister... Abba ji, this year you must make a movie with Nimmi... Which director do you want, sister... Just name it... Karan Johar, Subhash Ghai or Ram Gopal Verma...

Nimmi looks upset and walks out of the balcony. Abba ji looks at Kaka, who is speechless. He doesn't know what just happened.

KAKA

नई वैसे अपना मणि रत्नम भी ले सकते हैं...

Even Mani Ratnam would do... actually.

Cut to Abba ji's angry face.

SC. 17

INT. /DAY/CAR

Abba ji and Nimmi on their way to 'urz'. Nimmi asks the driver to stop the car.

NIMMI

रोको जरा...

Stop...

She takes off her slippers.

NIMMI

यहाँ से पैदल जाना है हमें... नंगे पांव...

I'm going to walk from here... barefeet...

ABBA JI

अंधेर खुदा का... बीबा... छाले पड़ जायेंगे...

God be kind... You'll burn your feet, dear...

NIMMI

वही दिखाने हैं उसे...

If that's what the Almighty wants...

ABBA JI

अब हम क्या करें...?

Now what do I do?

NIMMI

आप चलिए ना... गाड़ी में...

You come... in the car.

Nimmi leaves without bothering to listen.

ABBA JI

आपको अकेला छोड़ के...

I can't leave you by yourself...

Maqbool comes from the car following behind.

MAQBOOL

क्या हुआ अब्बा जी...

What happened... Abba ji?

ABBA JI

मियाँ... ये इश्क बहुत बड़ी बीमारी है... पूरी कायनात हमारी मुट्ठी में है... मगर एक बित्ते भर की औरत नहीं सँभलती... नंगे पांव जाएंगे दरगाह तक...

Love is the greatest disease in the world, son… the whole underworld's in my grasp… but this little runt of a woman I can't control…

MAQBOOL

आप चलिए मैं आता हूँ बी के साथ...(To the driver) चलो...

You carry on… I'll come with her…

Cars leave. Cut.

SE. 18

EXT. /DAY/ROAD

Maqbool joins Nimmi on her walk.

NIMMI

कौन है वो तुम्हारी हिरोइन...

Who's this heroine of yours?

Maqbool keeps quiet.

NIMMI

बहोत खूबसूरत है...?

Is she pretty?

Maqbool keeps quiet. Nimmi stops him and holds his hand.

NIMMI

हम से भी ज्यादा...

Prettier than me?

Maqbool frees his hand and walks forward. Nimmi joins him.

NIMMI

झूठ बोलता है तुम्हारा वो ज्योतिष इंस्पेक्टर पंडित... अब्बा जी की जगह तुम कभी नहीं ले सकते...

That astrologer Inspector Pandit of yours... he's a goddamn liar... You'll never take Abba ji's place...

Maqbool smiles.

MAQBOOL

क्यूँ...?

Why?

NIMMI

डरपोक हो तुम...

You're a wimp... that's why.

MAQBOOL

अच्छा...

I see...

NIMMI

हमरे इश्क में गल जाओगे लेकिन छूने की हिम्मत नहीं है... गुड्डू लेगा उनकी जगह... गुड्डू

Then what... you'd burn in my love but you'd never have the guts to touch me... Guddu is the real successor to Abba ji...

Maqbool smiles.

MAQBOOL

गुड्डू...

Guddu?

NIMMI

हँ... बेटा ना हो तो दामाद ही वारिस होता है...

If you don't have a son, the son-in-law becomes the next in line.

Maqbool stops. His expression changes.

MAQBOOL

गुड्डू दामाद... गुड्डू... समीरा... तुम्हें कैसे पता...?

'Son in law'... Guddu and Sameera... How do you know all this?

NIMMI

बस पता है...

I just do...

MAQBOOL

झूठ... झूठ ना?... झूठ ना...

Liar!

Nimmi smiles and looks straight into his eyes.

NIMMI

तुम्हारी हिम्मत नहीं होती थी हम पे निगाह डालने की फिर भी तुम्हारी नीयत मालूम थी हमें... बारह तिल हैं हमारे बदन में... कहाँ-कहाँ हैं... देखोगे... अरे मर सकते हो तुम हमारे लिए और... मार भी सकते हो... झूठ है ये...?

You never had the guts to even look at me but I knew what you wanted... There are twelve moles dotting my body... you want to see where all? You can die for me at this very instant... and kill for me as well... Tell me if that's a lie...

SONG 1 (*Tu mere ru baru hai*): *Sufi song starts at dargah. The singer is singing in the praise of the Almighty, but the impact is implying Maqbool's feelings for Nimmi, and Guddu's for Sameera. People tie threads for 'mannat'. We see Guddu and Sameera do so simultaneously. Maqbool catches this. Nimmi smiles. Song ends as their car leaves back for the town.*

SC. 19

EXT. /DAY/ROAD

A police jeep stops Abba ji's car. Purohit arrives at Abba ji's car, Maqbool also rushes. Abba ji lowers the window glass.

INSP. PUROHIT

सलाम अब्बा जी... आज आप वापस शहर मत जाइए...

Don't go back into the city today... It's not safe...

MAQBOOL

क्यूँ...

But why?

INSP. PUROHIT

मंत्री जी ने कहा दो दिन मे केस सुलटा देगें...

Bhosle's said he'll overturn the case in a couple of days...

KAKA

कौन सा केस...?

What case?

INSP. PANDIT

(whispers)

देवसरे ने अब्बा जी के नाम का वारंट...

Devsare's got a warrant issued in Abba ji's name.

Abba ji smiles.

ABBA JI

अब ये कोई उम्र है हमारी... भागने दौड़ने की...

This is no age for me to run about...

He asks the driver to proceed.

ABBA JI

चलो...

Drive...

Car leaves.

CUT TO:

SC. 20

EXT. /INT. /DAY/ABBA JI'S HAVELI

Abba ji's caravan stops. Devsare is waiting outside with a lot of police force. People have gathered around the house. Nimmi and Sameera go inside.

MAQBOOL

किसने लगवायी इधर गाड़ी?

Who's parked all these cars here?

Devsare avoids Maqbool and addresses Abba ji directly.

DEVSARE

जहाँगीर खान आपका नाम है?

Is your name Jahnagir Khan?

MAQBOOL

ऐ... कल सुबह आना... जमानत तैयार मिलेगी...

Come back in the morning... you'll have the bail papers in your hands...

Devsare avoids Maqbool and looks at Abba ji...

DEVSARE

जहाँगीर खान आपका नाम है?

Is your name Jahangir Khan?

Maqbool turns Devsare around.

MAQBOOL

अब्बा जी बोल बे... तेरे जैसे 36 वर्दी वाले पलते हैं हमारे यहाँ...

Call him Abba ji, you dick... we have three dozen cops like you hatching in our backyard...

Devsare avoids him again and turns to Abba ji.

DEVSARE

जहाँगीर खान आपका नाम है?

Is your name Jahangir Khan?

Maqbool turns Devsare around.

MAQBOOL

कितना चाहिए... घर पहुँच जाएगा... चलो...

How much do you need... we'll have it sent across... Now scram!

Devsare slaps Maqbool so hard that everyone freezes. Maqbool reaches for his pistol. Kaka keeps a calming hand on his hand. Abba ji goes quietly inside the jeep, while everyone stares in rage...

SC. 21

EXT. /DAY/POLICE HEADQUARTERS

The public is gathered around the headquarters. A car stops. Maqbool, Kaka and Guddu get off with a lawyer. Cut.

SC. 21A

INT. /DAY/POLICE HEADQUARTERS

Inside, the lawyer puts the paper in front of Devsare. Devsare doesn't bother to read it, he orders one of his subordinates to bring Abba ji. Maqbool pulls a chair and sits in front of him. Devsare looks at him and then asks others to sit.

DEVSARE

बैठिए...

Sit...

Abba ji arrives, looking as if he has hardly slept. He signs the release form. Devsare returns his pistol.

DEVSARE

आप जा सकते हैं...

You are free to go...

ABBA JI

सुबह का वक़्त है मियाँ... एक प्याली चाय भी नहीं पिलाओगे?

It's early morning, son... won't you offer even a cup of tea?

Devsare holds Maqbool's look and nods to ask for some tea. The mood changes. They all sit quietly watching him. The tea arrives. They sip it in silence. Just then a white Ambassador of the home ministry stops outside the headquarters. A man arrives with an envelope for Devsare. The four men watch in silence as Devsare reads his transfer orders. He looks at Abba ji.

KAKA

अरे... ट्राँसफर? कहाँ हुआ?

Oh dear! Transfer orders?? Where to?

ABBA JI

(smiles)

आप याद बहोत आयेंगे मियाँ... खुदा हाफिज़...

You'll always be in our thoughts… take care…

SC. 22

INT. /DAY/ABBA JI'S HAVELI

Kaka is trying to reason out with Maqbool while Abba ji is making his paan.

KAKA

अरे वो गया यहाँ से... अब नहीं आएगा वापस फिर क्यूँ उड़ाएगा उसका भेजा...

He's out of our hair… then why do you want to blow his brains out?

MAQBOOL

ठीक है... उसका दिल उड़ाउंगा...

Fine… I'll shoot him through his heart. Alright?

Maqbool looks at Kaka with fierce eyes. Kaka continues.

KAKA

देख... कोई नया राड़ा नई शुरू करने का अपने को अभी... भोसले कभी हामी नई देगा उसे उड़ाने की...

See… we can't afford a fresh row. Bhosle wants us to lie low.

Maqbool is hurt.

MAQBOOL

तो फिर मेरा लाफा खाएगा बीच बाजार में खड़ा होके भोसले... पूछ उसे...

Tell Bhosle I'll come there and slap him in public… Ask him if he'll like that…

Abba ji, who was listening to all this quietly, gets up and holds Maqbool's hand.

ABBA JI

आ... चल...

Come…

He brings Maqbool out on the street.

ABBA JI

ले, मार ले मुझे...

Here… slap me now.

Maqbool looks down.

ABBA JI

मार ना... तेरी आग तो बुझे मियाँ... वरना इस आग में हम सब जल के राख हो जायेंगे...

Slap me… give me all the anger you've got… else we'll all burn down in it…

Maqbool keeps looking down. Abba ji comes close to him and holds his hand.

ABBA JI

वो लप्पड़ आपको नहीं हमारे जहाँगीर के गाल पे पड़ा था... कल से रमज़ान है... ईद तक कुछ नहीं...

That slap stung me much more than it did you... Ramzan starts tomorrow... nothing doing till Eid...

Maqbool hugs Abba ji.

CUT TO:

SC. 23

EXT. /DAY/MOSQUE

Abba ji, Maqbool and the others come out of the mosque. It's Eid. Everybody greets each other warmly. Suddenly Palekar, the opposition politician, emerges from the crowd. He greets Abba ji as he extends his hand.

PALEKAR

अब्बा जी... ईद मुबारक आप सब को...

Abba ji... Eid greetings...

Abba ji greets him graciously and then excuses himself. Palekar proves difficult to shrug off.

PALEKAR

अब्बाजी... इस बार दाल-गोश्त नहीं पका हवेली में? भोसले बड़ा जलाता है उँगलियाँ चाट चाट के...

There's no feast at the mansion this year...? Bhosle keeps boasting about the grand meals that you host...

Abba ji's face screws up into a smile.

CUT TO:

SC. 22

INT./DAY/HAVELI

Abba ji sits on his swing, making paans as everybody else sits around, eating the sweets. Palekar among them.

ABBA JI

मीठी ईद है पालेकर मियाँ... बकरीद पे आइयेगा... गोश्त खिलायेंगें... सुपारी कैसी लेंगे? सूखी या गीली?

This is the Sweet Eid, Palekar… come join us for Bakr-e-eid next time… we'll feed you some juicy goat… how would you like your betel… wet or dry?

PALEKAR

जी नहीं मैं पान नही खाता...

No thanks… I don't eat paan…

Abba ji darts him a look.

PALEKAR

बुरा ना मानें तो एक बात कहूँ?

If you don't mind, can I share something with you…?

Abba ji nods.

PALEKAR

आप जेल गये... अच्छा नहीं लगा... भोसले चाहता तो रोक सकता था...

I didn't like the fact that you had to go to jail… Bhosle could've averted it if he wanted to…

Abba ji doesn't react, keeps making his paan.

PALEKAR

अब्बा जी बस आपका आशिर्वाद चाहिए... छे दिन में सरकार गिरा सकता हूँ... भोसले नंगा नाचेगा विधान सभा में... नंगा...

I just need your blessings, Abba ji… I can topple this government in six days… I'll strip Bhosle clean in the assembly…

Abba ji asks him to draw near. Palekar goes up close. Abba ji offers him the paan.

ABBA JI

खाओ...

Eat this…

PALEKAR

जी नहीं...

No, thanks…

ABBA JI

खाओ...

Eat it…

PALEKAR

मैं पान नहीं खाता...

I don't eat paan…

At which point, Abba ji takes the paan and stuffs it in his mouth violently. Palekar is too shocked to react. His PA tries to move but Kaka holds him back. Abba ji shoves it all the way in and then wipes his red-stained hand on his kurta.

ABBA JI

गिलौरी खाया करो गुलफाम ज़बान काबू में रहती है...

Get some good taste in your mouth… it helps keep your palate clean…

Palekar storms out in a huff, his PA following him. He turns to look back at Abba ji once. Maqbool, who was standing in the corner, taps him on the shoulder.

MAQBOOL

लाल रंग फबता है तेरे कुर्ते पे...

Red looks good on you actually...

Usman breaks out into raucous laughter on hearing this. Palekar's humiliation is complete.

INT. /DAY/FILM SET

A dance director is showing the dance steps of a mujra song to a heroine. Nearby her secretary is fighting with a producer.

SECRETARY

डार्लिंग गुस्सा नही होने का... मैं मैडम से बात करेगा...

Darling, don't get upset. I'll speak to Madam...

PRODUCER

दो दिन के लिए दो साल से wait कर रहा हूँ... अब तो Association में Complaint डालना ही पडेगा...

I've waited two years... for two days of shooting. Don't force me to lodge a complaint with the Association...

SECRETARY

डार्लिंग धमकी नई... No threat, हाँ...

Darling... no threats please...

Suddenly the secretary sees a man entering the studio gate. It's Thapa, Maqbool's man. Thapa ambles upto the producer.

THAPA

और क्या हाल है? मुँह लटका हुआ है? यार हमें भी बना दो हीरो...

What's up brother? Why so serious? Get me a good role somewhere...

The secretary runs upto Mohini and whispers something into her ear.

SC. 23A

EXT. /DAY/FILM SET

Cut to a car with a black window screen, outside the studio. Mohini comes out walking while the secretary is holding the umbrella for her. She stops in front of the car's black window screen. The window glass comes down. It's Maqbool. Mohini smiles.

MOHINI

जहाँगीर साब से कहिएगा हम पैसा नहीं देंगे... आप गोली मारना चाहते है तो मारिए...

Tell Jahangir sir, I don't have the money to pay up... If he wants to shoot me, he's most welcome...

She takes off her 'dupatta', exposing her cleavage. Maqbool looks away and puts his hand on the driver's shoulder. The car moves. Mohini smiles.

CUT TO:

SC. 24

EXT. /INT. /DAY/ABBA JI'S HAVELI

An official-looking person, who'll simply be known as the Professor, sits around a table with the members of the gang. Abba ji, Maqbool, Pandit, Purohit, Guddu, Boti are all present.

Abba ji sits at the head of the table.

PROFESSOR

रियाज ने बताया कि आप उसके वालिद की तरह हैं...

Riyaz (Boti) regards you dearer than his father.

Boti nods enthusiastically. Professor continues.

PROFESSOR

डील 30 करोड़ मे तय हुई थी मुगल से... सामान इंटरनेशनल वाटर्स की हद तक हमें लाना है... फिर हिन्दुस्तान के समन्दर से बम्बई तक लाने की जिम्मेदारी आपकी होगी...

The deal was struck for thirty million with Mughal. We'll carry the consignment till the edge of the international waters... Thereafter, you'll have to escort it till it lands here in Bombay...

MAQBOOL

इस्तेमाल कहाँ किया जाएगा... दिल्ली, कश्मीर या यहाँ पर?

Where will it be used? Kashmir, Delhi or here?

PROFESSOR

कहीं भी हो... मगर पैसा आपके घर तक पहुँचेगा... पूरा और वो भी काम से पहले...

Doesn't matter... But the money will reach you... all of it... And that too, before the job is done...

Guddu cracks up on hearing this.

GUDDU

सॉरी... आप धन्धा करने आये हैं या खुदकुशी... मतलब गड़बड़ हम करेंगे तो भी नुकसान आपका...?

Are you on some suicide mission or what? So, you pay us in full even if the plan doesn't take off...?

PROFESSOR

बेटा हर इंसान का मकसद फायदा नही होता... हमारी अब्बा जी की दोस्ती दरकार है...

Not everyone works for petty profit... We're here to build relations with Abba ji...

Abba ji gets up from his chair and comes and sits next to the Professor.

ABBA JI

(clasping Professor's hand)

शायद हम आपकी दोस्ती के लायक नहीं हैं प्रोफेसर साहब... हमारी क़ाबिलीयत हमारा कारोबार... और हमारे पैर जमीन पर है... तैरना भी नही जानते तो दरिया से दूर भले...

We are not worthy of your friendship, sir... Our business and our feet are firmly planted on land... Never learnt to swim... So it's best we stay away from the waters...

PROFESSOR

आप चाहें तो दुनिया के हर मुल्क मे आपका कारोबार फैल सकता है...

If you choose well today, your businesses could spread far and wide in the future...

Abba ji ponders for a moment.

ABBA JI

मुंबई हमारी महबूबा है मियाँ... इसे छोड़कर हम कराची या दुबई मे नहीं बस सकते... चाय...?

Mumbai is my sweetheart... Can't jilt her at this age and settle for Karachi or Dubai... Would you care for some tea...?

The meeting is over. Abba ji gets up from his chair. The Professor walks off, slighted. Boti follows him out.

KAKA

अब्बू तीस करोड़ रूपये... वो भी काम के पहले, अगर हम नहीं करेगें तो कोई और करेगा...

Thirty million in cash, Abba ji. That too before the deal goes through… If we don't do it, somebody else will…

ABBA JI

जिस इंसान का मकसद सिर्फ नुकसान हो उस से किसी का फायदा नहीं हो सकता... याद रखना...

He who doesn't care for profit can never be of use to anybody… Always remember this…

Abba ji walks out. As Guddu is making his way out, Maqbool accosts him.

MAQBOOL

हगना मूतना सीखा नही, धंधा सिखाता है? अबकी बीच मे बोला... तो ज़बान काट दूँगा साले..

Can't even piss in a straight line… and you are going to teach us how to run the business…? Next time you speak out of turn, I'll cut your tongue off…

He pushes Guddu hard who just stares back at him. Now Kaka screams at him.

KAKA

तेरी माँ का... आँख फोड़ दूँगा... भाग यहाँ से...

Sonuvabitch… stop glaring… Get lost!

SC. 25

INT. /DAY/ABBA JI'S BEDROOM (HAVELI)

Abba ji takes off his kurta while Nimmi lies in bed waiting. Like some prize catch. Abba ji starts making love to Nimmi.

His repulsively fat body moves over Nimmi. She looks totally uninvolved and keeps looking blankly.

SC. 26

INT. /DAY/LIVING ROOM OF HAVELI

Kaka is showing the model of a resort to everyone.

KAKA

नहीं नहीं नहीं, अंग्रेजी संडास से पेट साफ नहीं होता मेरा... मेरा बाथरूम मेरे को देशी चाहिए... चौड़ाके बैठने वाला...

I can't use an English lavatory... I need my Indian one... nice and easy to squat on...

Maqbool enters the courtyard.

KAKA

देखा मॉरिसस का रिसार्ट कितना ब्यूटीफुल है, नहीं? हमारे मियाँ का कमरा कहाँ है इसमें? ये देख तेरे को कोने मे ठहराएंगे साले...

Come Miyan... see the model of our Mauritius resort. Neat, isn't it? Which one is Miyan's room? Let's see... we'll give you the corner one...

MAQBOOL

अब्बा जी कहाँ हैं...

Where's Abba ji?

KAKA

सो रहे हैं...

He's resting...

Maqbool looks at his watch.

MAQBOOL

अरे अभी इस टाइम?

This time of the day? I'll go see...

Maqbool goes towards his chamber but Kaka stops him.

KAKA

ठीक है... भाभी के साथ है...

He's with her...

Maqbool hides his strain.

KAKA

अबे नींद और भूख का कोई टाइम थोड़ी ना होता है मियाँ...
कि होता है?

The kind of hunger that knows no time of the day...
You know which kind?

He chuckles hard. The others join in. We see the strained face of Maqbool. The sound of lovemaking fades in, overlapping the laughter.

CUT TO:

SC. 26 A

INT. /DAY/ABBA JI'S BEDROOM (Haveli)

Abba ji 's toad-like body towers over Nimmi's frame as Maqbool goes into a reverie. He starts hitting his head against the pillar. Suddenly there's some bustle and his vision is broken.

CUT TO:

SC. 26 B

Abba ji enters adjusting his pyjama cord. Everyone gets up to wish him.

EVERYONE

सलाम अब्बा जी...

Greetings, Abba ji…

ABBA JI

वालेकुम सलाम...

Greetings…

Abba ji stops and marvels at the model.

ABBA JI

माशाअल्ला बड़ा खूबसूरत है...

It's beautiful…

KAKA

वो थोड़ी गाडियाँ ज्यादा खड़ी की हुई हैं...

He's placed too many cars in the compound…
rest is great.

Abba ji has a bite of the paan. He calls out to Nimmi.

ABBA JI

बीबा सुपारी गीली नही है...

Dear… the betel is not wet enough…

Nimmi brings the paan box. Her hair is still wet. Her eyes meet Maqbool's. Abba ji talks to the architect while chewing his paan.

ABBA JI

साब ये हमारे आका है... इनकी मंजूरी के बगैर कोई फैसला
नही हो सकता...

Sir, she is the real decision-maker in this place… she needs to approve of the designs first…

ABBA JI

(to Nimmi)

बोलो बीबा... कैसा लगा ये?

Do you like it, dear?

NIMMI

अच्छा है...

It's not bad…

ABBA JI

अच्छा है? के बहुत अच्छा है?

It's good or it's not bad?

At that moment, Guddu and Sameera come running in, disrupting the conversation. Nimmi looks at them coldly.

NIMMI

माशाअल्ला!

It's great, actually!

Sameera looks excitedly at the model.

SAMEERA

वाओ! अब्बू मेरा कमरा कौन सा होगा?

Wow, Dad! This is amazing. Which of these is my room?

GUDDU

ये... मेरे पास वाला...

This one, right next to mine…

SAMEERA

अब्बू मैं इसके बगल के कमरे मे नहीं रहने वाली... बू से तो मर जाउंगी... छी...

Yikes! I'll die of the stench only...

ABBA JI

(to Maqbool)

मियाँ कुछ सोचा? कौन चलाएगा इसे? किसे भेजना है मॉरिसस?

Miyan! So then, who's going to run this resort? Who are we sending to Mauritius?

MAQBOOL

गुड्डू...

Guddu...

GUDDU

अरे नहीं-नहीं मुझे नहीं जाना... हुह...

I'm not going anywhere...

MAQBOOL

गुड्डू मॉरिसस जायेगा...

Guddu will go to Mauritius...

KAKA

गुड्डू क्यों भाई?

But why him?

MAQBOOL

गुड्डू जाएगा...

Guddu it is...

KAKA

अबे गुड्डू क्यूँ बे तू क्यूँ नही जाता...??

Who says so? Why does Guddu need to go? Why don't you go?

MAQBOOL

गुड्डू जाएगा...

I've decided... Guddu is the one.

Kaka turns him around.

KAKA

तेरी माँ का... एक लौंडा है मेरा... कहीं नई जाएगा वो...

Go stuff your decision... I've only one son and he's not going anywhere...

Maqbool is unfazed.

MAQBOOL

अब्बा जी गुड्डू मॉरिसस जाएगा...

Abba ji, Guddu will go to Mauritius. That's final.

Abba ji looks perturbed. The mood has changed. The other people get up and leave.

ABBA JI

क्यूँ मियाँ... गुडडू को क्यूँ भेजना है मॉरिसस...

What's up, Miyan? Why this hurry to pack off Guddu?

MAQBOOL

छोटी को गोद में खिलाया है मैंने... मेरी भी कुछ लगती है वो...

I've raised Sameera like my own child... she means something to me... doesn't she?

Everybody goes dead silent. Maqbool's words have scythed through the air, the words hanging heavy.

KAKA

मतलब क्या है बे तेरा...

What do you mean?

MAQBOOL

पूछ अपने चाँद के टुकड़े से पूछ...

Ask the apple of your eye…

Kaka charges towards Guddu.

KAKA

क्या बोल रहा है ये...

What the hell does he mean?

Guddu hangs his head and keeps quiet. Kaka charges towards him. He bashes the pulp out of Guddu, with whatever he can lay his hands on, abusing him like crazy.

KAKA

साला जिस थाली मे खाता है उसी में छेद करता है हरामी... कुत्ता भी दस घर छोड़ के मुँह मारता है...

Bastard… even a street dog doesn't piss ouside his master's house…

Nimmi is holding Sameera, who is crying and witnessing all this drama silently. Kaka keeps beating Guddu till he rolls and falls at Abba ji's feet. Sameera also slumps down. Guddu is bleeding profusely. Abba ji holds his face.

ABBA JI

बहोत चाहता है मेरी छोटी को... निकाह करेगा उससे...

You really love her? More than anything? Will you keep her happy?

Guddu lowers his eyes.

ABBA JI

फिर तो मक़बूल ठीक कहता है बेटा... तुझे मॉरिसस तो जाना पड़ेगा...
मेरी छोटी का घर इस कीचड़ में नहीं बस सकता...

Then Maqbool is right. You have to go to Mauritus...
My daughter's house can't bloom in this swamp...

Abba ji gets up after blessing them. A visibly relieved Kaka breaks down. He begs him for forgiveness.

ABBA JI

उठ उठ लड़की वाले तो हम हैं... समधी जी...

Now pick yourself up. We're going to be in-laws soon...

Kaka comes up to Maqbool and hugs him. He is fairly emotional and cries like a child.

KAKA

माफ कर देगा ना यार मियाँ... दोस्त हूँ तेरा पुराना यार...

Forgive me Miyan... for old times' sake.

Maqbool and Nimmi share a look. Nimmi, who is stunned by all that's happened, finds her voice. She chirps up.

NIMMI

हम तो कभी माफ नहीं करेंगे आपको... ये क्या शकल बना रखी है
आपने हमारे दामादजी की... अरे हमारे खानदान का वारिस है ये अब...
है ना?

But I'm never going to forgive you. Look what you've done to his face... The future heir of the family...

Nimmi hugs both Guddu and Sameera. Cut on Maqbool's strained expression.

SC. 27

INST./NIGHT/KAKA'S HOME

At night Kaka is nursing Guddu's back, which has gone blue after the beating. As he puts a hot towel, Guddu moans in pain.

KAKA

साले अगर अब्बा जी को तेरे इश्क की खबर कहीं और से लगती तो हम दोने गये थे आज...

If Abba ji had got wind of your affair from some other place… we'd both be dead by now…

GUDDU

चाहता तो वो भी यही था...

Exactly what he wanted…

Kaka hurls the food back in the plate. Guddu keeps quiet.

KAKA

साले कुत्ते... साले अहसान मान मियाँ का... अगर तू आज जिन्दा है ना तो सिर्फ उसकी ही बदौलत...

You bloody ingrate… you should thank Miyan instead… It's because of him that you're even alive today…

GUDDU

तू भी कितना भोला है रे बाबा...सांप और सपेरे मे फरक ही नहीं दिखता तुझे... उस हरामी के हलक से निवाला नहीं उतर रहा होगा आज...

Really Dad? You really think so… ? You still can't make out the snake from the snake charmer, can you? Maqbool must be in mourning today.

KAKA

साले...

You idiot…

Kaka raises his hand to him but stops.

KAKA

गोलियां खाईं हम दोनों ने एक दूसरे के लिए... समीर बहन बेटी है उसकी... तेरी जगह कोई और होता ना साले तो अब तक तेरी तेहरवी निपट चुकी होती...

Hush! we've taken bullets for each other... Sameera's like his own daughter... anybody else in your place would be buried in cement by now...

Kaka gets angry and goes to the window.

GUDDU

नाटक मत कर बाबा... खाना खा...

Relax, Dad... Come finish your food...

KAKA

भूख नहीं है...

Not hungry any more...

Guddu goes to him with a bite in his hand.

GUDDU

मेरे हाथ से...

Let me feed you...

KAKA

(turns)

देख गुड्डू छोटा सा परिवार है ये हमारा... इसमें जहर मत घोल... टूट जाएगा...

See son... this is all the family we have... Don't poison its roots... It'll break up...

Guddu takes the bit to his mouth and eats himself. Kaka smiles and hugs him. Guddu shouts in pain.

CUT TO:

SC. 28

EXT. /DAY/FARM HOUSE

The farmhouse is being given a fresh coat of paint. Labourers are decorating the exterior with flowers. Maqbool oversees the preparations.

MAQBOOL

चाचा अभी पीले वाले रहने दो... लाल लगाओ लाल...

Enough of the yellow flowers now... start on the red ones...

NIMMI

लगता है सारी मुंबई के बाग़ नोच डाले हैं तुमने...

Looks like you've mauled all the gardens of Mumbai...

A man brings some kababs on a plate. Maqbool tastes it.

MAQBOOL

तीखा है... कल कोई गड़बड़ नई चाहिए मुझे...

Too spicy... I don't want any slip-ups tomorrow...

CATERER

नहीं भरोसा रखिये...

Be assured, sir...

Nimmi's mobile rings.

NIMMI

जान... वालेकुम सलाम... देखिये ना जान...

तैयारी नहीं हुई है यहाँ... ये मियाँ आपका बातों का सौदागर है बस...

Greetings, dear… nothing seems to be ready here… your Miyan's been just lazing around…

Maqbool is shocked. Nimmi smiles and continues talking.

NIMMI

नहीं बिल्कुल नहीं... अरे ना फूल वालों का पता है ना खाने वालों का पता है...

No sign of the florists or the caterers…

MAQBOOL

अरे...

Hey…

NIMMI

खानदान की पहली मंगनी है जहाँगीर... नहीं हम हैं ना जान... अरे हम रूक जाएंगे यहाँ रात को जी... जी अच्छा सुनिये... कल ना दर्जी से हमारा शरारा जरूर लेते जाइएगा... हाँ अच्छा खुदाहाफिज़ जान...

It's the first wedding in the family, Jahangir. (*She listens to Abba ji on the other end.*) Don't worry now. I'll just stay back and get everything done. Just get my dress from the tailor's tomorrow.
See you.

She hangs up and looks at Maqbool. Maqbool holds her hand.

MAQBOOL

गला काट दूँगा तेरा...

I'll slit your throat…

Nimmi smiles.

NIMMI

अभी नहीं रात को...

Not now… later… At night…

CUT TO:

SC. 29

EXT. /DAY/SUNSET/TERRACE- FARM HOUSE

Maqbool is standing alone looking at the sea and sunset. A hand comes and takes out the pistol tucked in the back of his trousers. He turns instinctively and finds Nimmi holding the gun at him.

MAQBOOL

अरे क्या है यह... वापस दो...

What's all this? Give it back…

She opens the safety lock and smiles.

NIMMI

बोलो... वापस दो मेरी जाँ...

Say, 'Give it back, my love.'

Maqbool tries to take it and it fires in the air. Maqbool is startled, steps back. Nimmi mischievously smiles and pulls the trigger.

NIMMI

सच में मार दूँगी... मेरी जाँ बोलो...

I'll seriously do it… first say, 'my love'…

Maqbool, seething, whispers.

MAQBOOL

मेरी जाँ...

'My love'…

NIMMI
अहसान कर रहे हो... प्यार से बोलो ना मेरी जाँ...
You can do better than that... say it with some feeling, please.

Maqbool tries to cool his anger.

MAQBOOL
मेरी जाँ...
'My love'...

NIMMI
(laughs)
एक और बार...
Once more...

MAQBOOL
मेरी जाँ...
'My lurve'...

NIMMI
जाँ मेरी...
'Lurve of my life'...

MAQBOOL
जाँ मेरी...
'Lurve of my life'...

NIMMI
मेरी जाँ...
'My lurve'...

MAQBOOL
मेरी जाँ...
'My lurve'...

NIMMI

ठीक है... ठीक है मेरी जाँ...

Alright… alright… my love…

Nimmi laughs and gives the pistol back. Maqbool slaps her hard but she laughs more.

MAQBOOL

तू लखनऊ वापस क्यूँ नही जाती... रखैल कहीं की...

Why don't you just go back to where you came from? You whore…

Nimmi, still laughing, hugs him.

NIMMI

तुम साथ चलो तो लखनऊ क्या अल्लाह मियाँ के पास भी जाने को तैयार हैं हम...

If you're coming, I'm ready to go anywhere… even to the great beyond.

She laughs in such a manner that it brings a smile on Maqbool's lips too. She hides her face in Maqbool's arms and just laughs and laughs. Maqbool lifts her face, and sees it is full of tears. She hides her face and cries in his arms.

SONG 2 (*Rone do*): *The song starts. Maqbool lifts her in his arms and takes her into the bedroom. They make love, the whole night. The song, depicting Nimmi's emotions for Maqbool, plays in the background throughout the act.*

SC. 30

INT. /DAY/BEDROOM

Nimmi is praying, doing her namaaz. Maqbool is watching her. She finishes it and looks at Maqbool.

MAQBOOL

क्या माँगा दुआ में...

What did you ask for... ?

NIMMI

येही कि हर दिन इस रात सा बीते...

Every day should be like the night that passed...

MAQBOOL

अब्बा जी के जीते जी तो ये नहीं हो सकता...

Not till he's alive...

NIMMI

और अब्बा जी के बाद...

He won't live forever...

Maqbool reacts to this line, he looks into her eyes.

CUT TO:

SC. 31

EXT. /DAY/FARM HOUSE

A procession of cars arrives at the farmhouse. Abba ji and Sameera come out of one car, Kaka and Guddu from the other. Nimmi comes out and takes Guddu away.

NIMMI

चलो... चलो... मंगनी की रस्म से पहले तुम समीरा का मुँह भी नहीं देख सकते... समझे...

Go in... you can't see the bride's face till all the rituals are over...

She drags him inside, while everyone laughs. Abba ji shouts and asks.

ABBA JI

अरे मक़बूल कहाँ है...

Where the hell is Maqbool?

NIMMI

छत पे बिरयानी पका रहा है...

He's cooking biryani for everybody on the terrace.

SC. 32

EXT. /DAY/TERRACE

On the terrace, Maqbool, dressed like a 'bhatiyara', is cooking biryani in a very big vessel. Fresh spices are being pounded, a couple of small goats are tied nearby. Maqbool is giving intricate instructions.

MAQBOOL

अच्छे से पीसने का... क्या...इतने से लहसन में क्या होने वाला है मेलया.. .इतना ही और काटो...

ऐसे काटते हैं धनिया... बारीक काट बेटा... और थोड़ा सा लेके सिर्फ पत्तियाँ अलग करना...

Grind the spices well… this much garlic won't do… add some more… Goddamnit… is this the way to dice coriander?

He takes the knife and cuts some. He turns to the people working on the main vessel.

MAQBOOL

अरे हटो चाचा प्याज लग गयी...

Oh shit… my onion's getting singed…

He starts stirring the onion. Abba ji looks at all this with eyes full of love.

ABBA JI

अरे मेरे लख्तेजिगर... इधर आ...

Come here... my best man in the world...

He embraces the reluctant Maqbool, whose clothes are covered with spice stains.

ABBA JI

कितनी मोहब्बत से पका रहा है यार... जी करता है
अपना गोश्त पका दूँ तेरी बिरयानी में...

Seeing you cook with so much love... I'd readily cut my heart out and give it you.

Everyone laughs. Dholak beat starts. Cut to sangeet.

SC. 33

INT. /DAY/COURTYARD

Pandit and Purohit arrive for the function. As their taxi draws up, Purohit gives back to the cabbie his license.

INSP. PUROHIT

ये ले तेरा लाइसेंस...

Here, you can keep your license...

INSP. PANDIT

अब तो नही लगाएगा ना नो पार्किंग में गाडी...

Next time, watch where you park...

SC. 34

INT. /DAY /HALL - FARM HOUSE

Everyone has a beer mug in his hands. Insp. Pandit is opening the gift-wraps, while Purohit is explaining and showing the gift to others. He opens one gold bangle.

INSP. PUROHIT
कमिश्नर साब...
The Commissioner of Police...

A Rolex watch comes out next.

INSP. PUROHIT
और... बोटी... Rolex
Boti... Rolex.

INSP. PANDIT
इस घड़ी के साथ बोटी का बुरा वक़्त भी खत्म...
Hopefully he can put his bad times behind him now...

Everyone laughs. The next gift is a pair of keys.

INSP. PUROHIT

प्यारी समीरा को... एक 3 bedroom hall with lots of love...
अंकल भोसले...

'To my dearest Sameera... a small three-bedroom hall... With lots of love, Uncle Bhosle.'

Everyone is surprised.

KAKA

अंकल भोसले...

The great Uncle Bhosle...

ABBA JI

50 साल नेता बोतल मे बंद रखो फिर भी पूँछ सीधी नही होगी... gift भी सरकारी...

These politicians are cheapness personified... even their gifts are like government donations...

Everyone laughs again.

INSP. PUROHIT

पंडित जी और है? बस खतम...

That seems to be all...

MAQBOOL

आप दोनो खाली हाथ आ गए...

What about you two? Came emptyhanded again?

Everyone laughs again.

INSP. PANDIT

शुभ समाचार लाए हैं ना... देवसारे को काले पानी की सजा हो गई... कस्टम मे डाल दिया है उसे...

We got news... good news... Devsare's been banished to the high seas... they've put the bugger on customs duty.

Purohit whistles. Everyone laughs.

KAKA

अब्बू आपको याद है... आपकी शादी मे रेड हुई थी...

Abu... you remember... when the cops raided your wedding party...

Abba ji laughs.

ABBA JI

सेहरे से लेकर जांघिया तक उतरवा लिया था सालों ने... क्या नाम था कमिश्नर का...

The buggers frisked me from head to toe... removed everything from my turban to my underwear. What was the name of that commissioner?

KAKA

देशपांडे... देशपांडे... और लाल जी भाई ने अपने हाथ से भेजा उडाया था... उस हरामजादे का... अब्बू... अगर आज लाल जी भाई जिन्दा होते तो कितना खुस होते... नही...

Lalji Bhai later blew his head off with his own hands... I'm really missing him today...

ABBA JI

याद मत दिला काका... अनाथ लगता है हमें उनके बिना...

Don't go there, Kaka... I still feel orphaned without him...

Pandit smiles and looks at Purohit. Abba ji turns to Purohit.

ABBA JI

तुम लोग सालों.... किसी के सगे नहीं हो सालों... वो ACP मोर्या... सगे भाई से ज्यादा मानते थे उसे लाल जी भाई... छाती फाड़ डाली हरामी ने गोलियों से...

You guys are not to be trusted... that ACP Maurya... Lalji Bhai considered him his own brother... what did the bugger do? He riddled his chest with bullets...

KAKA

अब्बा जी नहीं... खुशी का मौका है... आज नहीं... आज नहीं...

Abbu... not today... Not on such a festive day...

Tears fill up in Abba ji's eyes. Nimmi enters.

NIMMI

आँसू पोछिए... मोहिनी जी आई हैं...

Wipe your tears... Mohini's here...

Everyone is surprised, and looks at Maqbool, who smiles back.

CUT TO:

SC. 35

INT. /NIGHT/DANCE HALL

SONG 3 (*Jhin min jhini*): *Mujra starts. Mohini dances and flirts with Abba ji. Kaka whispers to Maqbool.*

KAKA

अब्बा जी की नई बीबा...

Abbaji's new squeeze...

Nimmi looks from far at Maqbool. In one corner Pandit is chatting with Maqbool.

INSP. PANDIT

बच गया दिलीप कुमार...

Dilip Kumar must be thanking his stars...

Maqbool looks at him.

MAQBOOL

कैसे...?

What do you mean?

INSP. PANDIT

अंडरवर्ल्ड मे ना होते तो फिल्म स्टार होते... क्या एक्टर हैं अब्बा जी...
तीन लोग थे कमरे में... लाल जी भाई, ACP मौर्या और अब्बा जी...
जिंदा बचे ये... बेवफा कौन... पुलिस... कुत्ती कौन... पुलिस...

If he hadn't been in the underworld, Abbaji would have been a great film star… what an actor he is!! There were three people in the room… Abbaji, Lalji bhai and ACP Maurya… the only one who came out alive was Abbaji… So who are the real turncoats? The cops… ? Who are the real bastards? The police… ?

The caterer comes.

CATERER

कुर्बानी के लिए बुलाया है...

They're ready for the sacrifice…

SC. 36

EXT. /DAY/TERRACE

Nimmi is putting mehndi on the goat's forehead. She picks up one of the garlands and puts it around the goat's neck. She picks up another garland and turns to Maqbool and wears it herself. The servants take goats inside the bathroom.

NIMMI

हमारी भी कुर्बानी कर ही दो अब... जहाँगीर को उसकी नयी बीबा मिल गयी है...

It's time you sacrificed me too… Jahangir's got his new mistress…

Tears fill up her eyes. She turns her face.

NIMMI

(while crying in a choked voice)

किस मुँह से घर वापस जाऊं... सबको पता है जहाँगीर की रखैल हूँ मैं...मेरे बाप की उम्र होगा वो कम से कम... नंगा कितना घिनौना लगता है... बू आती है उसके बदन से मुझे...

Can't even go back home… Everyone knows I'm Jahangir's concubine. He looks so repulsive naked… must be as old as my father.

She wipes off her tears and turns to Maqbool and looks at him with firm eyes.

NIMMI

जो होगा आज रात होगा... एक को मरना होगा... तुम्हें... हमें... या जहाँगीर...

You'll have to kill one of us… it's either you, me or Jahangir…

The heads of the goats are cut inside the bathroom, blood flows out of the drain hole.

CUT TO:

SC. 38

INT. /NIGHT/BAR ROOM

Abba ji and Mohini raise their glasses. Everyone is around.

ABBA JI

क्या फरमा रहीं थी आप...

So what were you saying?

Mohini looks at Usman, Abba ji's bodyguard.

ABBA JI

अरे ये मक़बूल का घर है... माँ के पेट की तरह महफ़ूज़ है... जा... 25 साल से साथ है... मै आज जिंदा हूँ तो इसकी बदौलत...

Relax Usman… this is Maqbool's house. Safe as a womb… now go drink some milk…

MOHINI
I don't believe it.

ABBA JI
ऐ उस्मान... कमीज़ उतार अपनी...
Come here... take off your shirt.

Everybody is amused.

MOHINI
Striptease...

Usman smiles and refuses.

ABBA JI
ऐ... शर्माने का नही... उतार
Go on... take it off.

As Usman takes off his shirt everyone claps. His whole body has innumerable bullet marks.

ABBA JI

कान्दला बाले किस्से में 6... भयखला मे 3... कोल्हापुर मे 4... एक गोली छू भी नहीं सकी हमें... आज तक...

Turn around... those six in Kandla... three in Byculla... four in Kolahapur. Not a single one of those could touch me...

Everyone claps. Abba ji goes emotional.

ABBA JI

एक राम का हनुमान थे, एक जहाँगीर का उस्मान है...

Ram's disciple was Hanuman, Jahangir's Usman...

Everyone laughs.

ABBA JI

हँसने की बात नही है... कुछ भी कर सकता है ये हमारे लिए... कुछ भी...

He can do anything for me.

NIMMI

(smiles)

अच्छा... कुछ भी...

Anything? Really?

ABBA JI

(looks)

कुछ भी...

Anything...

Nimmi puts a bottle of rum in front of him.

NIMMI

पियो...

Drink this...

Usman refuses. Nimmi looks back at Abba ji and shrugs her shoulder.

ABBA JI

पियो उस्मान...

Drink it... Usman...

Usman looks down. Abba ji starts to get angry.

ABBA JI

बोतल उठा उस्मान...

Drink it... Usman...

Usman looks at Abba ji from the corner of his eyes.

ABBA JI

(shouts)

उस्मान

Usman...

Usman picks up the bottle. Everybody claps as he gulps down the bottle. Abba ji gives a devilish smile to Mohini. Maqbool and Nimmi exchange a look.

CUT

SC. 38

EXT. / NIGHT / LAWNS

Pandit and Purohit are drinking Black Label in the lawns. Pandit has made the horoscope chart on the table with 'namkeen'.

INSP. PUROHIT

चिंचपोकली की Black Label लगती है... साली चढ़ती ही नही... शादी में हम लेंगे दारू का contract.

The Black Label seems to be from Chinchpokli... dosen't fucking go to the head... For the wedding we will take the liquor contract...

INSP. PANDIT

शादी...?

Wedding...?

Pandit laughs softly, Purohit reacts.

INSP. PUROHIT

क्या हुआ...?

What happened...?

INSP. PANDIT

लड़की मंगली है... बहुत लाशों पे से विदा होके जायेगी...

The girl is cursed... She will leave behind a trail of corpses before she is wed...

Purohit smiles and gulps down his drink.

CUT TO:

SC. 39

EXT. /DAY (MAGIC HOUR)/TERRACE

The ropes that tied the goats are lying on the ground. The blood on the floor is being washed into the drain. The family Nanny is supervising the ferrying of the food vessels. Maqbool is standing in a corner, pensive. A storm is brewing as winds lash the open terrace.

NANNY

कैसी अजीब रात है... ये बारिश ये मौसम... 70 साल में पहली बार...
चलो... या अल्लाह क्या मर्ज़ी है तुम्हारी?

Such strange weather... In my seventy years, I've never seen it rain in this month... Lord have mercy...

As they leave, Nimmi walks upto Maqbool.

NIMMI

तय किया तुमने?

Have you decided?

MAQBOOL

हम...

Hmm?

Maqbbol takes out his gun and puts it on her temple. She doesn't flinch. He pulls the trigger. It's a blank. Nimmi eyes open in a smile. Maqbool smiles back. The heavens open up just then.

SC. 39A

EXT. /INT. /NIGHT/FARMHOUSE

Pandit and Purohit staring heavenwards as it pours. Everybody eating and making merry in the central courtyard. Guddu and Sameera feed each other from the same plate. We see Usman in a corner, still drinking and getting high. Nimmi takes Abbaji inside to sleep. He gives Mohini a good night kiss.

SC. 40

Pandit and Purohit, completely drunk, pissing on the wall.

INSP. PUROHIT
शक्ति का संतुलन बहुत जरूरी है
Power is game of exquisite balance...

INSP. PANDIT
आग के लिए पानी का डर बना रहना चाहिए...
You need water to balance out the fire...

INSP. PUROHIT
Ready...

INSP. PANDIT
Steady...

Both – go!

They start making designs on the wall, seeing who can shoot furthest. Maqbool on the terrace is watching this from a distance.

He turns around to see that the blood in the corner has still not been washed off. He shouts for someone.

MAQBOOL
रामजु... अहमद...
Ramzu... Ahmed...

A help comes running.

MAQBOOL
यह खून साफ क्यों नहीं किया अभी तक...
Why has the blood not been washed off?

AHMED

साफ तो है बाबा...

It's been washed, sir...

He looks at the floor again and this time, there is no blood.

MAQBOOL

ठीक है जाओ...

Fine... leave...

The help scurries off. Maqbool looks back at the floor and sees fresh blood again. He's losing his mind.

SC. 41

INT. /NIGHT/CORRIDOR

In the middle of the night, Maqbool comes out dressed in his night clothes.

SC. 41A

INT. /NIGHT/FARMHOUSE VARIOUS

Maqbool slowly walks across the lawn. Flashes of Abbaji's lovemaking with Nimmi jostle with his own memories of her. The music grows to a fever pitch and suddenly comes to a complete stop. Maqbool is standing outside Abbaji's room. Usman is drugged out. Maqbool steals Usman's pistol and sneaks into the room.

SC. 41B

INT. /NIGHT/ABBA JI'S ROOM (FARMHOUSE)

Nimmi is wide awake. Maqbool stands over the bed. They look at Abbaji, who is in deep slumber. A moment of decision as they lock eyes. Maqbool removes the silencer and fixes it over

Usman's pistol. He tears his eyes away as he pulls the trigger. Blood splashes on Nimmi's face as the bullet pierces through Abbaji's heart. A beat. Suddenly, Abbaji's eyes open and he clambers out of bed. Maqbool and Nimmi are paralysed with fear. Abbaji tries to get up but crumples into a heap on the floor, lifeless.

SC. 41C

Cut outside as Maqbool places the gun in Usman's hand, back in position.

SC. 41D

Back inside, Nimmi takes out Abbaji's gun from underneath his pillow. In the still night, we see Nimmi at the window. She points the gun in the air and shoots.

SC. 41G

Outside Abbaji's room, the drugged Usman wakes up with a start. Blindly, on instinct, he picks up the gun in his lap and blunders into the room.

SC. 41H

Inside the room, Nimmi is waiting calmly with the gun pointed at the door. Usman looks confused. Nimmi shoots him in the chest.

SC. 42

There is a furore in the house as people start rushing towards Abbaji's room. Maqbool is the third to enter. They stop and stare at the dead Usman with the gun in his hand, and Nimmi, still shivering, holding up Abbaji's gun. Fade out.

INTERMISSION

SC. 46

EXT. /DAY/FARM HOUSE

A line of cars dots the dusty terrain. Maqbool's caravan stops outside the farmhouse. A boy shouts from the terrace, announcing their arrival. The gunmen run outside the house and take position. Maqbool's men get off the cars and do the same. It's a Mexican stand-off. Maqbool coolly gets down from his sedan and walks towards the gate. He takes out his gun and drops it to the ground. He asks his men to wait outside.

CUT TO:

SC. 47

INT. /DAY/FARM HOUSE

Maqbool and Thapa enter the courtyard. Kaka, Guddu and Boti sit around, serious. Nobody greets him. Maqbool's eyes meet Boti's. Maqbool opens his arms to embrace Kaka. Kaka refuses.

MAQBOOL

काका...

Kaka...

KAKA

वापस जा...

Go back...

Maqbool tries to put his hand on Kaka's shoulder. Kaka shrugs him away.

KAKA

मत... छू मत... तेरे से बोला वापस जा... वापस जा साले...

Don't touch me... just go...

Kaka storms off. Maqbool follows him. Guddu comes in the way. Maqbool stops for a while and pushes him away. On cue, Guddu's men take out their guns. Maqbool looks at them, eyes blazing. He turns to Guddu.

MAQBOOL

भाईयों के बीच में कोई आएगा नहीं...

I'm going to speak to my brother and nobody's going to come in our way...

He goes to the roof. Kaka stands in a corner, crying.

MAQBOOL

काका ओये काका...

Kaka...

Kaka turns, his eyes red.

KAKA

क्या मिल गया तुझे अब्बू की जगह लेके साले?

What did you get by getting rid of Abba ji?

MAQBOOL

वही तो मै भी जानना चाहता हूँ काका क्या मिला मुझे... 25 साल कुत्ते की तरह साली वफादारी की... गोली खायी गले काटे... यह दिन देखने के लिए... तू भी यही सोचता है कि अब्बा जी को...

You tell me... would I kill somebody I served like a dog for twenty-five long years... I could kill for him... even die for him if he'd asked... and even you think I killed him... ??

Kaka wipes his tears.

KAKA

पता नहीं...

I don't know anything any more...

Maqbool turns Kaka around and punches him on his face. Kaka falls on the ground. He charges towards Maqbool in anger. Maqbool takes out a small Mauser, tucked in his undershirt, and puts it on Kaka's forehead.

MAQBOOL

अब बोल... पता है कि नहीं...

Now tell me... do you know or not?

Kaka is fuming out of anger and helplessness. Guddu and Boti enter, cocking their guns. Maqbool is all fury as he threatens to pull the trigger.

MAQBOOL

अब बोल... पता है कि नहीं...

Look here... do you know or not?

He suddenly takes Kaka's palm and puts the gun in it. Kaka is surprised. Maqbool opens his arms.

MAQBOOL

इधर देख... इधर देख काके... इधर देख... या तो गोली मार या गले आ के मिल...

Look here... do you know or not? Now either shoot me or come hug me...

Kaka staggers ahead and embraces Maqbool. He just cries and cries in his arms. Guddu is not happy with this turn of affairs.

CUT TO:

SC. 48

EXT. /NIGHT /

Sameera is sitting next to the balcony in her room, looking sadly at the faded colour of mehndi on her palms. Tears rolls off her eyes. Maqbool comes from the back.

MAQBOOL

बहुत हो गया ये रोना-धोना... सामान बाँध और जाने की तैयारी कर...

That's enough mourning for a lifetime... pack your bags... You're leaving...

Sameera is surprised.

MAQBOOL

गुड्डू आ रहा है... कल नियाज़ पे...

Guddu's coming for the memorial service tomorrow...

A ray of hope shimmers in Sameera's eyes, which are full of tears.

CUT TO:

EXT. /CHINNA'S HOUSE/DAY

Pandit, Purohit and Chinna are sitting around. A religious ceremony is going on in the background.

Purohit closes his fingers and shows him his fist.

INSP. PUROHIT

यह क्या है सोचो...

What is this, brother?

Chinna looks askance.

INSP. PUROHIT

शक्ति... पावर...

Strength... Power...

He now opens the fist and spreads his palm.

INSP. PUROHIT

और यह क्या है...

And this... ?

INSP. PANDIT

भिखारी का कटोरा...

A begging bowl...

They both chuckle at their own joke.

INSP. PUROHIT

अन्ना... टाइम मे साथ मिल के रहने का है...

This is the time to stay united... brother...

SHETTY

चालीस दिन हो गये... अब तक नही पता चला कौन था...

It's been forty days... we still don't know who did it...

CUT TO:

SC. 45

INT. /DAY/SALOON

Pandit and Purohit chat up Tawde inside a salon.

INSP. PANDIT

भई कमरे में तीन लोग थे... अब्बा जी... उसमान और...

There were three people in the room...
Usman, Abba ji and...

Purohit hides a smirk as Pandit stops mid-sentence.

INSP. PANDIT

खैर का नियाज़ है... जो मक़बूल को क़बूल नहीं करेगा वो कातिल...

Anyway, tomorrow's the service. Whoever doesn't turn up for it, is the murderer...

Tawde, who's getting a face massage, pipes up.

TAWDE

सुना है निम्मी और मियाँ साथ सोते हैं...

Is it true Nimmi and Maqbool are sleeping together?

INSP. PUROHIT

भाऊ... वो साथ सोते है साथ जागते है उसका धंधे से क्या लेना देना...

That has nothing to do with the business, brother...

INSP. PANDIT

धंधे के उसूल से तो... अब्बा कि हर चीज अब मियाँ की है... चाहे बेटी हो चाहे रखैल...

And the rules of business dictate that whatever was Abba ji's once, is now Maqbool's to keep… be it daughter or whore…

CUT TO:

SC. 49

INT. /DAY/MAQBOOL'S ROOM

Maqbool is praying, doing the namaaz. Nimmi enters, looks furious.

NIMMI

मियाँ...

Miyan…

Maqbool does not respond and keeps on praying.

NIMMI

सपोले को दूध मत पिला मियाँ... दाँत निकलते ही तुझे डसेगा सबसे पहले...

Miyan… don't usher the snake in… he'll be the first to bite you…

Maqbool completes his prayers and opens his eyes.

MAQBOOL

नियाज़ की तैयारी हुई?

Is everything ready downstairs?

NIMMI

गुड्डू इस घर से हमारी लाश पे से चल कर आएगा शाम को...

Guddu will have to walk over my corpse to enter this house...

Maqbool looks up at Nimmi.

MAQBOOL

शाम होने तो दे निम्मा...

We'll see who walks over whose corpse...

Nimmi looks into his eyes. Maqbool's eyes have the smile of a ruthless animal.

NIMMI

आयतें याद है तुम्हें...

You know all the prayers by heart?

MAQBOOL

हाँ... क्यूँ...

Ya... why?

NIMMI

पहले कभी देखा नहीं ना नमाज़ पे... बहुत मासूम लगते हो...

Never seen you in prayer before... you look like a baby...

She hugs him tightly.

CUT TO:

INT. /HAVELI/MORNING

Maqbool, Shetty, Boti, Tawde and others sit in a pensive mood at the dining table before the peace prayers for Abba ji begin.

MAQBOOL

मैं कोई जोर ज़बरदस्ती से ये जगह नहीं ले रहा हूँ... किसी को कुछ बोलना है तो बोले... अभी मुझे बोले...

I have not taken this authority by any force... If anyone has anything to say, speak now...

TAWDE

काका और गुड्डू नहीं आये हैं अभी...

Kaka and Guddu have not arrived yet...

MAQBOOL

तू अपना बोल...

Speak for yourself...

SHETTY

देखो मियाँ तुझ में हम सब को विश्वास है... हम सब को... इसी दिन की ताक में बैठा है पालेकर... एक फूट पड़ी नहीं कि सरकार गिर जाएगी... और मिल कर रहे तो जय महाराष्ट्र...

Miyan, we all have faith in you… All of us… Palekar is looking for an opportunity, one crack and he will topple our government… If we are united then Maharashtra stays united, Hail Maharashtra…!

CUT TO:

EXT. /INT. /CAR/HIGHWAY

Kaka and Guddu travel to the haveli with their henchmen. Guddu looks upset and turns up the music. Kaka kicks the system shut. Guddu lashes out at his father.

GUDDU

ठंड रख बाबा... तेरी वजह से चल रहा हूँ मैं समझा... जा माथा टेक मंदिर में...

Calm down, old man. It's only because of you that I'm going there. Now, go and pay your respects…

The car stops outside an old temple by the road. As Kaka leaves, Guddu calls out.

GUDDU

और सुन... कुछ बुद्धी माँग ले अपने लिए...

And ask God to knock some sense into your senile head…

As they wait around, one of the men comments that Kaka's been gone too long. Suddenly, there's an attack on their cavalcade. Kaka dies in the ambush. Guddu retaliates but he is outnumbered. He somehow manages to give the attackers the slip and escapes.

SC. 50

INT. /DAY (LATE EVENING)/HALL

The prayers for Abba ji start at Abba ji's haveli. At home we see everyone including Minister Bhosle, Chinna, Tawde, Boti,

Nimmi and Sameera and all other gang members. Sameera is looking at her watch impatiently. Maqbool prays for Abba ji's soul.

MAQBOOL

अल्लाह अब्बाजी की रूह को सुकुन पहुँचाये उन्हें जन्नत नसीब करे...

Wherever he is... he should accept our prayers.

The maulvi puts a hand on Maqbool's head to bless him. The fumes from the incense sticks float towards Nimmi, making her uncomfortable. The maulana continues with his prayers when suddenly Nimmi shrieks. Maqbool's eyes open.

NIMMI

मियाँ...!!

Miyan...!!

Maqbool and the others turn around. Pandit and Purohit walk in, carrying the bloodied body of Kaka into the courtyard. There is a collective hush as everybody is shocked.

INSP. PUROHIT

मियाँ... काली के मंदिर में...

Found him at the temple...

INSP. PANDIT

माता के सामने...

Right in front of the mother goddess...

INSP. PUROHIT

जिन्दा था लेकिन अस्पताल पहुँचते पहुँचते...

He was still alive but didn't make it to the hospital...

INSP. PANDIT

रास्ते भर बुदबुदाता रहा... हवेली पे चल... हवेली पे चल...

Kept blabbering all the way... 'Take me to the mansion...'

CHINNA

कौन था

Who did it?

MAQBOOL

कौन था? कौन होगा? हरामी जना था साले ने... अरे काके!

Who the hell do you think it was? That bastard son of his... who else??

TAWDE

गुड्डू... नरक मे भी जगह नही मिलेगा कुत्रया को...

Guddu... that dog won't even get a place in hell...

Everybody's shocked at Maqbool's accusation but nobody says a word. Sameera runs inside, crying. Maqbool bends down to have one last look at Kaka. Suddenly Kaka's dead eyes open. He turns his face and looks straight at Maqbool. Maqbool is shocked to the core. He stumbles back, his eyes pale with fear.

MAQBOOL

ले के जाओ उसको यहाँ से... यह जिंदा है... आँख खुली उसकी... इसको लेके जाओ यहाँ से...

Take him away… he's alive. Why did you get him here? Take him away.

Nimmi tries to calm him down. Everybody is looking at Maqbool now as he shivers with fear.

NIMMI

मियाँ... मियाँ... मर गया है काका... मर चुका है वो... मर चुका है काका... मियाँ...

He's dead, Miyan… See, he's not moving. Kaka's dead.

Maqbool looks again. Kaka's lifeless body lies on the ground. Maqbool gets conscious of the surroundings and composes himself.

CUT TO:

SC. 51

INT. /NIGHT/POLICE VAN

Purohit and Boti are drinking inside the van parked in front of a temple.

BOTI

चूतिया बनाता है साला... अपने बाप को उड़ायेगा कोई?

He thinks we are all dunces… Who in his right mind would kill his own father?

INSP. PUROHIT

इतना ज्यादा याद मत किया कर बाप को... वक़्त से पहले वरना उसके पास पहुँच जाएगा...

Don't miss your dad so much... you might just meet
him before your time.

Pandit has a thali in his hand and puts tika on Purohit's forehead and turns to Boti. He slowly whispers while putting the tika.

Fear emerges in Boti's eyes. Purohit asks in a firm tone.

INSP. PANDIT

गुड्डू कहाँ है...

Where is Guddu?

Boti is quiet. Purohit takes out Boti's gun. Boti is shocked. Purohit asks the driver to leave.

The gate of the van is also closed.

INSP. PUROHIT

बोल बता दे... बता दे कहाँ है गड्डू...?

Don't be such a diva... tell us where Guddu is.

BOTI

नहीं पता... मुझे नहीं पता...

Don't know… I swear.

Purohit puts the barrel inside his nose.

INSP. PANDIT

सच...?

Really… ?

Boti is scared but quiet. Pandit smiles.

BOTI

सच... मुझे नहीं पता...

Really… I don't know…

INSP. PANDIT

अब्दुल चाचा के यहाँ? मैमन मुहल्ला में?

At Abdul Chacha's … in that old Muslim neighbourhood… No?

Boti turns with a jerk. Driver stops the van.

INSP. PUROHIT

ए गाड़ी रोक... चल उतर नीचे...

Get off…

Boti is trembling out of fear. He gets down from the van.

INSP. PUROHIT

चल भाग...

Now scram…

INSP. PANDIT

चल... चल भाग...

Move it… run.

Boti runs for his life. We stay on Boti's back, which is wet with sweat. Suddenly Boti falls but he quickly gets up and starts running harder than ever. We can hear Pandit shouting 'भाग...भाग' *(run... run) at a distance. Boti gets out of sight but no shots are fired.*

INSP. PUROHIT

छोड़ क्यूँ दिया उसे...

Why the hell did you let him go?

INSP. PANDIT

(smiles)

शक्ति का संतुलन बहोत जरूरी है संसार में... आग के लिए पानी का डर बना रहना चाहिए...

Power is game of exquisite balance... You need water to balance out the fire...

CUT TO:

SC. 52

INT. /NIGHT/BED

Nimmi is lying calmly inside the quilt and Maqbool is brushing her hair. He stops and asks:

MAQBOOL

इस बार महीना हुआ तुम्हारा...

Have you had your period this month?

She opens her eyes with a jerk and looks at him.

CUT TO:

SC. 53

INT. /DAY/ABBA JI'S HAVELI

Maqbool is sitting on Abba ji's place and making a paan for himself. Pandit is showing him the horoscope chart.

INSP. PANDIT

मियाँ आपका गुरू कर्क राशी मे आ गया... अब आपका कोई कुछ नही उखाड़ सकता...

Your stars have entered the House of Jupiter... nobody can dare touch you now...

MAQBOOL

और गुड्डू... उसको ढूँढ के निकालो... जल्दी...

What happened about Guddu? Hunt him down... I want that bugger...

Nimmi enters running with an envelope in her hand, calling Maqbool's name

NIMMI

मियाँ... मियाँ... मुबारक हो...

Miyan... congratulations...

She looks cheerful. Nimmi lovingly slaps Maqbool with the envelope, forgetting Pandit and Purohit's presence.

NIMMI

बाप बनने वाले हो तुम...

You are going to become a father...

Pandit and Purohit get up and congratulate Maqbool.

PANDIT + PUROHIT

मुबारक हो मियाँ...

Congratulations, Miyan... !

As they leave she puts his hand on her stomach.

NIMMI

तीन महीने का है...

It's already three months old...

Maqbool's expression changes. He pulls his hand back.

MAQBOOL

तुम आखिरी बार जहाँगीर के साथ कब सोई थीं...

When was the last time you slept with Abba ji?

Nimmi's smile vanishes. She tries to hide the rage in her eyes. Maqbool is numb, he frees his hand and tries to move. Nimmi holds him again.

NIMMI

तुम्हारा है मियाँ...

It's yours, Miyan...

Maqbool frees himself and walks out. Nimmi runs and holds Maqbool.

NIMMI

तुम कहो तो गिरा देते हैं इसे...

We'll get rid of it if you want...

She cries and hides her face in his arms. Maqbool gently pats her down.

CUT TO:

SC. 54

INT. /NIGHT/SAMEERA'S ROOM

Sameera opens the door and finds Maqbool standing in front of her. Sameera's eyes are red as she has been crying for hours. Maqbool gently embraces her. She does not respond.

MAQBOOL

बहुत याद आ रही है गुड्डू की? अब्बा जी को मारा है उसने... हमारे अब्बा को... मैं ज़बान देता हूँ छोडूंगा नहीं उसे...

Still thinking about Guddu? He's killed your father... our father... I promise you I won't leave that bastard...

There is hate in Sameera's eyes for Maqbool. She does not believe him. She has a smile on her lips ridiculing his concern.

MAQBOOL

मै तेरे लिए उससे भी अच्छा लड़का ढूंढूंगा...

I'll find a better match for you...

Maqbool leaves. She closes the door, her eyes full of tears, runs towards her bed, puts her face in the pillow and starts howling. She takes out Guddu's photograph and looks at it while crying. The music fades in.

SONG 5: *The song of separation starts, discovering the relationship of Guddu and Sameera. The complete montage starting from their childhood to falling in love. The time lapse.*

Fade out.

SC. 55

EXT. /DAY/OLD MUSLIM NEIGHBOURHOOD

Pandit has spread the kebabs on the bonnet of his van as he predicts the charts. Purohit goes to eat one but Pandit ticks him off.

INSP. PANDIT

अये अये... शुक्र मत खा... मंगल ले...

Hey, hey! … don't eat Venus… here… eat Mars…

Purohit smiles and goes to pick another.

INSP. PANDIT

अबे क्या कर रहा है यह शनि है...

What the hell… That's Saturn…

INSP. PUROHIT

अगर यह शनि मैं खा लेता तो क्या हो जाता...

What if I'd eaten Saturn up?

INSP. PANDIT

आदमी शनि को नही... शनि आदमी को खाता है...और इन दिनों बहुत भूखा है यह...

We don't eat Saturn… Saturn eats us, and these days it's famished…

INSP. PUROHIT

किसे खाएगा...

Who is it going to eat?

INSP. PANDIT

किसे खिलाना है...

Who do you want eaten?

They both chuckle. Just then a car drives up. The window comes down, we see Palekar inside, dressed in civvies.

PALEKAR

साब... यह नासीर का ढाबा कहाँ है?

Excuse me... do you know where Nasir's hotel is?

INSP. PANDIT

मियाँ कबाब खाना है तो अबदुल के ढाबे में खाओ... दुआ दोगे हमें...

If it's kebabs you're after, try Abdul's eatery... you won't be disappointed...

Palekar smiles. The car moves on.

INSP. PANDIT

संतुलन बन रहा है...

The balance of power... it's shifting.

CUT TO:

SC. 56

INT. /DAY/ABDUL'S EATERY

Palekar sits opposite Guddu and Boti at a ramshackle eatery. He is chomping kebabs as he speaks.

PALEKAR

सीख ना हो... तो कबाब कैसे भूनोगे... हुह... औ तुम तो यह भी जानते हो... उस घर मे गोश्त खान से आता है... बकरे खान काटे है...

Without a proper skewer, you can't make kebabs as good as this... plus you know everything about that house... where the goats are bled... where the meat comes from...

Palekar turns to address the waiter.

PALEKAR

चाचा बहुत बढ़िया... और एक प्लेट... और चटनी ज्यादा कांदा कम...

Good stuff, Man... get me one more plate of this... and less onion and more chutney.

PALEKAR

बस एक मक़बूल है जो गेम पलटा सकता है... सिर्फ छे दिन... सिर्फ छे दिन मे सरकार गिर जाएगी... नंगा नाचेगा भोसले विधान सभा में...

Maqbool is the only person who can foil this plan... If you guys back me, I'll topple this government in six days flat... Bhosle will be stripped naked in the assembly a week from now.

BOTI

हमें क्या मिलेगा?

What will we get in return?

PALEKAR

माँगने तो मैं आया हूँ तुम्हारे पास... तुम मक़बूल की टंगड़ी काटो... मै मुंडी पे लगता हूँ...

Listen... I'm the one who's come here asking... let's join hands... you cripple Maqbool's businesses from down to up... I'll start working from up to down.

SC. 57

INT. /DAY/SALOON

Tawde is in his favourite barber's chair, getting ready for his shave. Suddenly he feels something sharp at his throat. A smear of red trickles out. Tawde screams out at the attendant.

TAWDE

देख के बना साला...

Watch where you're going...

His voice trails off as he sees Guddu standing above him with the blade glistening in his hand. Cut to Tawde's ghostly expression.

INT. /NIGHT /MAQBOOL'S HOUSE

Maqbool picks up the phone in the middle of the night. The scene is intercut between Chinna and Maqbool.

CHINNA

हेलो... हेलो... मियाँ... थाना पनवेल अमबरनाथ कालबा... हर जगह पे टारगेट हुआ...

Miyan... Thana, Panvel, Kalba, Ambarnath... each and every stronghold of ours has been ambushed...

CHINNA

अपना तावड़े भी ऑफ हो गया..

They got Tawde too...

Maqbool gets out of bed with a start. Nimmi's not next to him.

MAQBOOL

कौन था? किसने किया...

Who was it? Who did all this?

SHETTY

पता नही.. भोसले की भी..

No idea... Bhosle's also in deep shit...

Maqbool hears Nimmi crying somewhere. He follows the sound. He can't hear what Chinna is saying anymore.

MAQBOOL

निम्मी... निम्मी... (back to Chinna) क्या?

Nimmi... Nimmi... (back to Chinna) What were you saying?

SHETTY

भोसले की भी चोरी हुइ है... 15 MLA गायब है उसके... बुलाया है आपको अभी...

Fifteen of his MLAs have gone missing... Bhosle's called for you right now.

Maqbool reaches the balcony and finds Nimmi sitting in a corner, sobbing.

MAQBOOL

निम्मी!... सुन तू सम्भाल... मै नही आ सकता...

Nimmi!... you guys handle it... I can't come right now.

He shuts the phone. Chinna turns to his henchman and cries out in despair.

CHINNA

मियाँ... उस राँड के चक्कर मे सबको मरवाएगा साला...

That whore will be the death of us all...

The henchman shoots Chinna in mid-sentence and walks out.

SC. 55A

EXT. /NIGHT/BALCONY

Nimmi sobs quietly as Maqbool lifts her face.

MAQBOOL

क्या हुआ?

What happened, dear?

Nimmi looks totally stressed, her eyes have a manic air about them.

NIMMI

नहीं सोने देता हमें...

Won't let me sleep...

MAQBOOL

कौन

Who?

Nimmi slaps her stomach.

NIMMI

ये...

Him...

Maqbool smiles and lovingly pats her stomach.

MAQBOOL

अये... अये... खबरदार... हैरान करता है तू हमारी जान को... हुं? चलो सो जाओ अच्छे बच्चे की तरह... एकदम...

Shush... Don't harass my sweetheart... go to sleep like a good baby... sleep now...

Nimmi cries louder.

NIRNMI

नई नई नई सोएगा यह... हमेशा रोते रहता है... रोते रहता है...

No... he won't sleep... keeps wailing all the time.

Maqbool brushes her hair.

MAQBOOL

तुझे सुनाई देता है पगली...

Dodo... you can hear him cry or what?

NIMMI

हाँ... दिन रात हमें इसका रोना सुनायी देता है... इसके बाप को मारा है ना हमने...

Ya... I can hear him cry all day... we killed his father, after all...

Maqbool's eyes go cold. He slaps Nimmi hard.

MAQBOOL

इसका बाप जिंदा है भी... यह बच्चा मेरा है... समझी...

His father is alive... this is my child... get that inside your bloody head...

Nimmi curls up in fear.

CUT TO:

EXT./ DAY/GUEST HOUSE

A news report announces that the government is in trouble. The ruling party has accused Palekar of hijacking fifteen of their MLAs and taking them to an undisclosed location.

A posse of journalists has converged upon the entrance as Palekar's PA fends off their questions.

PALEKAR'S P.A.

शांत हो जायें... शांत हो जायें... अरे नहीं भाई नहीं... देखिये देश कि सेवा करते करते थक जाते हैं... यह भी तो इन्सान ही है ना... कोई जोर ज़बरदस्ती नहीं लाया गया है... आराम करने आए हैं... होलीडें... वे देखिए... वे देखिए कितना उल्लासित हैं...

Calm down please... see... even they get tired of working day in and day out. After all, everybody's human. Nobody was forced... they've just come for a little R & R... See... how happy they all look.

The cameras train themselves on the politicians, basking in the sun, on the terrace. They all wave at the cameras.

This is being viewed on TV by Bhosle and Maqbool. Camera travels inside the house and catches them sitting quietly. Maqbool shakes his head.

MAQBOOL

30 करोड़??!

30 crores??!

Bhosle puts some ice cubes in his drink.

BHOSLE

हाँ... 30 खोखा... अगर सरकार बचानी है... तो पालेकर का डबल देना पड़ेगा...

Ya... 30 crores... if we are to save the government, we have to pay double of what Palekar's offering...

MAQBOOL

चिन्ना तावड़े ऑफ हो गए हैं... फैमली को दुबारा बनाने में थोड़ा वक़्त लगेगा ना भाऊ...

Chinna, Tawde have been snuffed out... I'll need time to rebuild the gang.

Bhosle changes his tone.

BHOSLE

और अगर पालेकर पावर मे आए न... तो सवसे पहले तू अन्दर जाएगा तू... समझा...

If Palekar comes to power, you'll be the first to be hauled behind bars...

Maqbool is at his wit's end.

MAQBOOL

अभी तीन दिन में कहाँ से आएगा 30 करोड़?

Now, where do I get 30 crores in three days' time?

Bhosle finishes taking a sip of whisky.

BHOSLE

अपनी निम्मा से जा के पूछ...

Why don't you go ask your Dear Nimma?

Maqbool loses it and charges towards Bhosle. Bhosle smiles and grabs his hand.

BHOSLE

ये तेवर वहाँ दिखा जहाँ जरूरत है... समझा...

Go show this anger where it's really needed...

Cut to Maqbool's face. The worry lines are loud and clear.

CUT

SC. 60

INT. /DAY/POLICE STATION

Purohit is torturing a criminal who is hanged upside down in the lock-up. Maqbool enters the police station with his men. Some havaldars try to stop him. He slaps one so hard that he bangs into the wall, others leave the way. Maqbool enters inside the lock-up and holds Purohit's stick. Purohit is zapped.

INSP. PUROHIT

मियाँ आप यहाँ... मुझे बुला लिया होता...

Miyan... you here! You should have just called for us.

MAQBOOL

मक़बूल की बाँबी में किसने हाथ डाला है...?

Who has dared to mess with Maqbool's domain?

Purohit falls on his feet.

INSP. PUROHIT

मियाँ मैं वही पूछ रहा था इस साले से... ये कुछ उगलता ही नहीं मियाँ मैं क्या करूँ...

I don't know Miyan... honestly... I was asking him the same thing... but he doesn't squeal...

MAQBOOL

कौन था?

Who was it?

INSP. PUROHIT

मियाँ मैं इतनी देर से पूछ रहा हूँ साला कुछ बोलता ही नही है... तुम्हारे सामने पूछा हूँ मैं... मियाँ तुम्हारे सामने पूछा हूँ...

I swear Miyan... I have no idea... I've been asking this sonuvabitch for the last three hours... bugger just won't spill...

Suddenly Purohit gets up, takes the gun from the havaldar and starts beating the criminal brutally with its butt.

He reverses the gun and shoots the criminal. He turns to Maqbool with folded hands.

Maqbool puts the gun on his forehead again.

MAQBOOL

कौन था?

Who was it?

INSP. PUROHIT

जल्दी पता चल जाएगा मियाँ... जल्दी पता चल जाएगा...

We will find out very soon, Miyan… very soon…

Pandit's voice comes from the corner.

INSP. PANDIT

गुड्डु और बोटी अब बच्चे नही रहे मियाँ...

Guddu and Boti are not kids any longer…

Maqbool walks towards Pandit who has made the horoscope on the floor with the blood of the shot criminal. Maqbool sits against the horoscope.

INSP. PANDIT

सारा दोष राहु और चंद्रमा का है...

It's all the moon's fault…

INSP. PUROHIT

नही... अब्बा जी का ही, खुद तो चले गये और बोटी को छोड़ गये हमारे मियाँ की कबर खोदने के लिए...

No… it's Abba ji's fault… He let off Boti to prepare Miyan's last rites…

INSP. PANDIT

पिछले 2 महीने मे साले चंदा मामा ने स्थिति बदल ली है... तीन दिन बाद ग्रहण है... बस ये टल जाए...

The moon has been really fickle these last two months… there's an eclipse in three days' time… we should bide our time till that passes.

MAQBOOL

30 खोखा चाहिए मुझे... तेरे इस ग्रहण से पहले...

I need thirty crores before your eclipse appears…

Everyone is stunned. Purohit whispers to Maqbool.

INSP. PUROHIT

कितना?

How much… ?

CUT TO:

SC. 61

EXT. /NIGHT/BEACHFRONT

Pandit has made a giant horoscope on the sand. Purohit chomps away at a cob.

Maqbool sits at the head of the chart. Pandit smiles and looks into the horoscope.

INSP. PANDIT

80 साल पहले पड़ा था ऐसा ग्रहण... बड़े बड़े डूब गये थे...

80 years back, an eclipse of this proportion appeared… it swept away the best of the best…

MAQBOOL

मै डूबूँगा की बचूँगा...

Will I sink or swim?

INSP. PUROHIT

बचोगे मियाँ बचोगे... डूब कैसे सकते हो... पुलिस तुम्हारे साथ है... भोसले तूम्हारे पीछे है... रहा गुड्डु और बोटी... सुवह तक दोनों की लाश तुम्हारे कदमों में पड़ी होगी... नही तो बोदी कटवा दूँगा साली...

Who has the gall to sink you Miyan? Bhosle's behind you… the cops are with you… That leaves Guddu and Boti… If I don't grab them by tomorrow, I'll shave my head off…

Maqbool turns to Pandit.

MAQBOOL

ओके... मैं डूबूँगा की बचूँगा...

Will I sink or swim?

INSP. PANDIT

(smiles)

अब दरिया खुद चल के तेरे घर आएगा मियाँ तो तू डूबेगा...

If the sea comes into your house, obviously you'll sink...

INSP. PUROHIT

दरिया चल के आएगा? पैदल आएगा कि गाड़ी में...

The sea will come... how... by car or on foot?

INSP. PANDIT

क्यों हवाई जहाज से भी आ सकता है...

Why? It can even take a private jet?

INSP. PUROHIT

दरिया घर पे आएगा...दरबाजे पे घंटी बजाऐगा...

The sea will come... press the door bell and announce itself...

INSP. PANDIT

डिंग डाँग डिंग डाँग।

'Ding Dong... Who's there?'

INSP. PUROHIT

हैलो... मियाँजी घर पे हैं?

'Hello everybody... is Miyanji at home?'

INSP. PUROHIT

कौन?

'Who is it?'

Suddenly Purohit gets serious.

INSP. PUROHIT

मैं हुं जी दरिया...डुबाने आई हूँ... बडी दूर से आई हुँ... दरिया आऐ... डुबाने आऐ...

'I'm the big blue choppy sea... I have come from far to sink the whole lot of you...'

इससे पहले के दरिया तेरे घर मे घुस जाऐ... तू दरिया के घर मे घुस जा...

The sea is coming to get you, Miyan... before the sea enters your house, you enter his...

SC. 62

EXT. /DAY/OUTSIDE MAQBOOL'S HOUSE

A procession of cars descends on Maqbool's house. There is a surprise attack led by Guddu and his men. There is a stand-off between them and Maqbool's men. The Nanny meets Guddu at the door.

NANNY

गुड्डु... तू कहाँ चला गया था? हमारी याद भी नहीं आई तुझे... बिटिया आधी हो गई... चल बेटा...चल अंदर चल...चल अंदर चल ना...

Where were you all this while? You didn't think of us once? The girl is at the end of her tether... come... now what are you waiting for?

A bullet catches her in mid sentence. She slumps to the floor. All hell breaks loose as bullets starts to fly from both directions. Finally, Maqbool's men are silenced. Guddu and his men enter the courtyard. Sameera runs out and embraces Guddu. She cries in relief. Just then Nimmi opens the door, Guddu is shocked to see her state. She seems completely senile. She comes forward and smiles at Sameera.

NIMMI

ए छोटी ले आ गया ना तेरा राँझड़ा... कितना रोती थी पगली...

There he is, sweetheart… now stop that mad howling and screaming…

Sameera pushes her hand away.

SAMEERA

छू मत मुझे डायन...

Don't touch me, witch…

NIMMI

क्या हुआ... ऐसे क्यूँ बात कर रही है हमसे...

Why are you behaving like this?

Sameera pushes her hand away and cries.

SAMEERA

मेरे अब्बू का खून पिया है तूने, चुड़ैल है तू...

You've drunk my father's blood, that's why, you witch…

She picks up a spade and tries to kill Nimmi. Guddu holds her hand.

GUDDU

बच्चा बेमौत मारा जाएगा पेट मे...

The child will needlessly die in the womb…

Sameera drops the spade and looks at Nimmi with disgust. Guddu looks at Nimmi,

GUDDU

वैसे माँ कहलाने के लायक है नहीं तू... राँड...

You don't deserve to be a mother though, you whore!

Nimmi rubs her face vigorously as they leave. Guddu and Sameera walk out of the house, through the line of corpses. Nimmi slides to the ground, broken.

CUT .

SC. 64

EXT. /DAY/BEACH

Maqbool stands before the ocean, staring at its silent strength. It's a pleasant, sunny day. A boat sails up, a plank is dropped and Maqbool gets in, staring at the gently lapping water all the time.

SC. 64A

INT. / EXT. /DAY/CUSTOM BOAT

Purohit, a customs officer, the coke man, Salvekar, and Maqbool on the deck of a custom ship. The customs officer is explaining on a map.

CUSTOM OFFICER

अगले एक हफ्ते तक यहाँ का पेटरॉल मेरे कमान्ड में है... कान्दला से 30 नौटिकल माइल नार्थ की तरफ...

This area is under my command for the next one week... right from Kandla till 30 nautical miles north...

MAQBOOL

पैसा...

Money... ?

KARIM BHAI

डिलिवरी पर...

On delivery...

Everybody goes tense. Maqbool looks at Pandit and Purohit. Professor senses the mood.

PROFESSOR

अब जरूरत आपकी है... दरिया में कारोबार करने आए हैं... पहले तैर के दिखाए....

Now the need is yours... First show me that you can swim... then we'll see about the money.

Pandit assures Maqbool to go with it. Maqbool gets a call on his mobile. The signal is not clear, he goes outside. The weather has changed. The skies have darkened and the waves are building up an angry fury. Maqbool listens to the voice at the other end. His face goes dark.

SC. 65

EXT. /INT. /DAY/HOSPITAL

Maqbool's car drives into the hospital. The doctor shows Maqbool a small baby kept inside an incubator. Maqbool caresses Nimmi's hair gently.

DOCTOR

48 घंटे तक ख़तरा है...

We can't say anything for the next 48 hours...

Maqbool looks back at the doctor with blank eyes. Outside the room a doctor is trying to stop Maqbool's man from entering.

DOCTOR

Visitors को आना मना है सर... I'm sorry...

Visitors are not allowed, sir... I'm sorry...

His man tries to wave at Maqbool, who does not notice. The man shouts loudly.

MAQBOOL'S MAN

मियाँ...

Miyan...

It breaks the silence of the hospital, but the voice does not reach Maqbool as the chamber is soundproof. We cut inside. Maqbool is brushing unconscious Nimmi's hair.

DOCTOR

It's a miracle, sir... बरना जिस हालत में इन्हे यहाँ लाया गया था...

It's a miracle, sir... considering how precarious her condition was...

Maqbool's man slaps the doctor outside very hard and enters inside.

MAQBOOL'S MAN

मियाँ... बोटी...

Miyan... Boti!

CUT TO:

SC. 66

INT. /NIGHT/ TAXI

Maqbool, Thapa and their men travel in silence. Thapa keeps his gun ready.

INT. /NIGHT/SEEDY HOTEL

Maqbool and his men attack the hotel. Each and every man of Boti's gang is killed in the gun fight. Maqbool and his men take position outside Boti's room. Maqbool smashes the door in.

Boti's son is playing with a toy gun while the wife is cowering on the bed. There is no sign of Boti. Maqbool reaches out to grab the child. Boti's wife protests while Thapa and the others comb the room.

BOTI'S WIFE

नहीं... नहीं...

No, please let him be...

Maqbool picks up the child in his arms.

MAQBOOL

अब्बू कहाँ है?

Where's daddy? Where did he go?

The child points towards the balcony. Maqbool walks out. He sees a limping Boti escape through the back street. The darkness swallows him up. Maqbool comes back in and looks at the wife, eyes breathing fire.

SC. 69

EXT. /NIGHT/BEACH

A small fishing boat is being laden with huge wooden boxes. Thapa supervises operations as the workers move the goods. Just as the last of the boxes is loaded, the sea is bathed in the glare of a spotlight. It is a coast guard boat. The men freeze. A megaphone blares at them to stop the boat and surrender. The boat comes closer and we see Devsare at its helm.

SC. 70

INT. /NIGHT/HOSPITAL

Maqbool enters the hospital in the middle of the night. He enters the ICU. He disconnects the glucose drip attached to Nimmi's wrist. The doctor tries to stop him.

DOCTOR

क्या कर रहे हैं ये आप... don't you know she's serious... what are you upto?

What the hell are you doing?

MAQBOOL

मेरे बच्चे को जिंदा रखना... बापस लेने आऊँगा...

Keep my child alive... I'll come back for him.

Maqbool picks up his Nimma in his arms.

DOCTOR

लेकिन यह मर जाएगी... ऐसा क्या हुआ है...?

Why are you risking her life like this? What has happened?

Maqbool turns and whispers.

MAQBOOL

दरिया घुस आया है मेरे घर में...

The sea has come into my house...

The doctor does not understand. Maqbool leaves.

CUT TO:

SC. 71

INT. /NIGHT/BHOSLE'S HOUSE/

Bhosle is playing a board game with his son. He gets a call from Maqbool who is driving with the semi-unconscious Nimmi on the backseat.

BHOSLE

हाँ बोल मियाँ...

Yes, Miyan...

MAQBOOL

नाव डूब गयी बाऊ...

My ship is sinking...

BHOSLE

सरकार भी...

So is the government...

MAQBOOL

कस्टम मेरे पीछे है बाऊ...

The customs guys are hunting for me...

BHOSLE

तो भाग...

Then you better start running...

MAQBOOL

तू दोस्त था यार...

You were my friend once, brother...

BHOSLE

हूँ... अब्बाजी का...

I was... Abba ji's friend.

Bhosle hangs up.

CUT TO:

EXT. /NIGHT/ROAD

Maqbool sees a police check-post. He rolls the window down. It's Inspector Purohit. He looks at Maqbool and whispers.

INSP. PUROHIT

हम अभी भी तेरे साथ हैं मियाँ...

We're still with you... Miyan...

He looks at the sky and takes a deep breath.

INSP. PUROHIT

आज रात का ये ग्रहण टल जाये बस...

Just let this eclipse pass tonight.

Maqbool's car leaves. A jeeps stops, Pandit jumps out of it and runs to Purohit in anger.

INSP. PANDIT

अबे क्यूँ छोड़ दिया उसे...

Why did you let him go?

INSP. PUROHIT

(smiles)

शक्ति का संतुलन... आग के लिए...

The balance of power...

Pandit concurs quietly.

INSP. PANDIT

पानी का डर बना रहना चाहिए...

Fire must fear water at any cost...

SC. 72

EXT. /INT. /NIGHT/FARMHOUSE

Maqbool and Nimmi arrive at the farmhouse; it is deserted except for a few guards standing around in the shadows. Maqbool and Nimmi enter through the door. She winces in pain as Maqbool struggles to carry her. It is dark. Suddenly music can be heard in the main hall. As Maqbool watches transfixed, a light comes on and we see the hall decorated with lights and flowers, filled with happy people, dancing and singing. We see Abbaji, dancing. Kaka, Usman and the Nanny give him company. Kaka cracks a low joke and laughs.

Maqbool shakes himself out of the reverie. Suddenly the hall is dark again.

CUT TO:

SC. 73

INT. /NIGHT/FARMHOUSE ROOM

Maqbool places Nimmi on the bed, and starts putting money, guns and bullets in a leather bag. He takes out two passports, checks them. Nimmi opens her eyes.

NIMMI

कमरा कब से साफ़ नही किया ये...

This room has not been cleaned in ages...

Maqbool looks at her, goes close and kisses her on her forehead. Nimmi gets up with a jerk.

NIMMI

सब... खून जम गया है दीवारों पे मियाँ कैसे छूटेगा अब...

See... the walls are still stained with blood. How will it all come off?

Maqbool turns; the walls are absolutely clean.

MAQBOOL

कहाँ...?

Where?

She turns him to the same site.

NIMMI

वहाँ... दिखता नही तुम्हें...

There... can't you see?

We see the wall full of the patches of black blood, from her point of view. Suddenly she looks at the bedsheet. It also has dry blood on it.

NIMMI

अल्लाह... चादर भी नही बदली तब से... हटो अरे हटो...

Oh God... even the sheets have not been changed...

She jumps off the bed and goes to the bathroom shouting aloud, while Maqbool looks at her in complete shock.

NIMMI

मुफ़्त की रोटी तोड़ते हैं नौकर सारे के सारे कोई खयाल नही है साफ़ सफ़ाई का... क्या करते हैं पूरा दिन...

These servants are all good for nothing... Who the hell is in charge of keeping all this clean?

She comes out carrying a bucket of water. He tries stopping her but she screams and pushes him away.

NIMMI

हटो मियाँ धोने दो हमें... धोने दो हमें अरे सड़ान आती है खून की मियाँ धोने दो हमें... वरना नींद कैसे आएगी रात को...

The stench of blood is everywhere… I have to clean up. I won't be able to sleep otherwise.

She starts washing the room. He loses the grip of the passports in his hand. They fall on the floor. He sits down with the support of a wall and watches her in helplessness. After a while she gets irritated, scratching a patch of the wall, and throws the cloth away and cries out. She comes and sits next to Maqbool.

NIMMI

अल्लाह मियाँ... हम पागल हो रहे हैं ना...?

I'm going mad, no?

Maqbool keeps quiet.

NIMMI

पागल हैं ना हम...

Tell me… I'm going mad, no?

She lies in his lap.

NIMMI

मियाँ... क्या सब गुनाह था मियाँ... सब कुछ... हमारा इश्क तो पाक था ना... इश्क तो पाक था ना... बोलो ना... बोलो ना...

Miyan… was everything a sin? Everything? Our love was pure… no? No?

Maqbool just cries and holds her tighter.

NIMMI

इश्क पाक था ना हमारा... मियाँ... बोलो ना मियाँ...

Our love was pure… no? Just tell me once…

Maqbool cries like a child in her arms.

VISUALS FADE OUT.

EXT. /INT. /DAY /FARMHOUSE

FADE IN.

It's morning. Devsare and his men enter the farmhouse. They creep up stealthily, surrounding the whole place. Just then, Pandit and Purohit's jeep drives up.

DEVSARE

तुम दोनों यहाँ क्या कर रहे हो? चले जाओ यहाँ से...

What are you two doing here? Get out of here…

INSP. PUROHIT

सर यह हमारा एरिया है सर...

This area falls under our purview…

Devsare just pushes them away and pulls his gun on them.

DEVSARE

I said shut up and get lost from here… I said move… come on quick… fast.

Pandit and Purohit hurriedly sit in the jeep and drive away.

Cut to Maqbool's room. Maqbool wakes up from all the commotion. Nimmi still lies in his lap. He gets up and looks at the men in white, crawling like ants. Maqbool walks back to the bed, takes a sheet and covers Nimmi. We realize she is dead. He hugs her one last time.

SC. 74B

INT. /DAY/FARMHOUSE/VARIOUS

Devsare and his men comb the house thoroughly. The whole place is deserted. From the roof, he catches a glimpse of a police jeep pulling away in the distance.

DEVSARE
Damn it...

SE. 75

EXT /DAY /HOSPITAL

Pandit and Purohit stop the jeep outside the hospital. Pandit whispers, while looking out.

INSP. PANDIT
मियाँ जरा जल्दी आना... फ्लाइट का टाइम हो रहा है...
Come soon... your flight's on schedule.

INSP. PUROHIT
सँभल के मियाँ...
Take care, Miyan...

CUT TO:

SE. 75A

INT. /DAY HOSPITAL

Maqbool steals into the hospital. He keeps a low profile, milling with the crowd. Just as he comes in, he sees Guddu entering the elevator. He goes for his gun but the doors shut. Maqbool runs up the stairs, gun in hand. Finally, he reaches his floor. Guddu is walking down the corridor. Maqbool follows with his gun.

When he reaches the ward, he looks in through the glass window. The doctor takes the child from the incubator and hands it to Sameera. She takes the child in her arms and looks up at Guddu. Guddu takes the child and kisses his forehead. Maqbool staggers, and we see the fight has gone out of him. His eyes brim over. He sees his son, in the arms of his loving guardians. He drops his gun and walks out in a daze.

CUT TO:

SC. 76

EXT /DAY /HOSPITAL

Maqbool walks out of the hospital. He brushes past Boti at the entrance, who takes a moment to realize who he is. He stops, shocked. He draws his gun, in full view. People stop and stare, transfixed; others run off in horror. Boti keeps shouting for Maqbool to turn and look at him, but Maqbool carries on walking, oblivious to him. Finally, Boti shoots.

Maqbool collapses on to the cold cement. As he lies dying, his eyes close gradually, shutting out the harsh sun. Life's fitful fever has come to an end.

The End